# Lord Ouseley

Football in England in 2014 looks to be diverse as we see more women, disabled and black, Asian and other minority ethnic players participating in the game, both in the professional sector as well as at grassroots level. But, we should not delude ourselves that opportunities in the game as a whole are accessible to everyone at all times.

Nowadays, as we become more immersed in a changing demography where we are likely to mix each day with people from different backgrounds, we are gradually becoming much more sensitive to the personal and collective responsibilities we have to treat each other fairly and not discriminate or abuse other people. Our institutions and organisations are required to ensure that opportunities are available to everyone, irrespective of their race, ethnicity, gender, sexuality, disability, religion or belief.

Sport, as a whole, offers opportunities, in theory, for inclusive participation. However, some sports remain uniquely exclusive and elitist. Football is an exception because you see the game being played by people of all ages on the street, on the beaches, housing estates, school playgrounds, back gardens, parks and open spaces and in some of the best stadiums around the world. Whatever your social background, personal characteristics or economic circumstances, there is the opportunity to play and it is particularly heartening to see more opportunities for girls and women and disabled people to participate.

Diversity in football demonstrates the power and capacity to bring people from different backgrounds together, to challenge bigotry and stereotypical views about some people and it has proved to be an effective way of getting to know about each other and contribute to social cohesion. Black people have suffered discrimination and exclusion for centuries in Britain and have been the victims of race hatred. This was reflected on the football pitches for over the past century or more and prominent black players have been at the forefront of putting up with racial abuse, overcoming discrimination, promoting race equality and breaking down the walls of ignorance that perp

But, while the players who are profiled in this book have made their contribution to this transformation and their visibility suggests that football is truly multi-cultural, there is a paucity in their presence as coaches, managers, administrators, board members and decision-makers which tells a story of continuing discrimination and exclusion.

This book helps us to reflect on an array of talented individuals who have provided entertainment with their skills and endeavour on the fields of play. It helps us to reminisce about their athleticism, their struggles, their commitment and contributions. It also reminds us how much more there still is to be done to utilise their talents and abilities in other aspects of the game where their invisibility remains part of the narrative of exclusion and denial.

**LORD HERMAN OUSELEY**
Chairman – Kick It Out

# Jim Cadman

This year sees the 125th Anniversary of Arthur Wharton signing for Rotherham in 1889 to become the world's first black professional football player.

Our book reviews the past 125 years and looks at the heritage created by over 50 individual black footballers, many of whom ignored the relentless racism of the football terraces and through self-motivation became role models and mentors for future generations of young black footballers.

Although I have provided the concept and the framework for this book I have been supported with the research, the sourcing of images, the collection of memorabilia and writing of copy by a dedicated support team.

This team includes students from Sandwell College who are drawn from over 90 countries throughout the world and represent a diversity of racial, ethnic and socio-economic backgrounds.

We could not hope to provide a definitive history of each player in the space available but we do hope that it will stimulate readers to look further into the careers and achievements of individual players and to investigate further the important role played by black players in our football heritage.

The publication of this book was made possible by a grant from the Heritage Lottery Fund whose support has been invaluable.

**Jim Cadman - October 2014**

**Contributors**

John Homer, Robert Endeacott, Chris Green, Tony Matthews, Ian Rigby

Sandwell College

Staff

Steven Powell, Hannah Randall, David Waldron

Students

Beatrix Ajetunmobi, Stephen Berry, Lauren Blakemore, Katy Burgess, Joanna Cash, Hannah Castle, Salaffina Dore, Eve Dube, Baylee Element, Alexandra Fogarty, Kyle Francis, Eleanor Gill, Katie Hughes, Sophie Jones, Arun Kalwan, Jonathan Kibbler, Viktoria Kohajdova, Kadar Muse, Freddie Mutambu, Rebecca Parker, Rebecca Reed, Tiffany Rowe, Tiffany Sankey, Connor Skidmore, Rebecca Smith, Dalian Watson, Christine Wood.

Photographs and Images

Tom Roe, Laurie Rampling, The Football Association, The National Football Museum, Bob Bond, Cyrille Regis, Paul Trevillion, Howard Talbot, John Cross, Les Gold, Kick It Out.

First published in the UK by the Sandwell Sporting Heritage Foundation 2014

ISBN 978-0-9560756-3-5    © Cornerstone Marketing Limited 2012

Publication concept devised and created by Cornerstone Marketing Limited. All rights reserved.

The rights of the contributors have been asserted in accordance with the Copyright, Designs and Patents Act 1998.

The publisher and contributors have made every effort to contact all copyright holders. Any errors that may have occurred are inadvertent and anyone who for any reason has not been contacted is invited to write to the publisher so that full acknowledgement can be made in subsequent editions of this book.

This publication would not have been possible without the input and contributions of the following people and organisations.

Design and artwork ©Crown Creative. Email: paul.burns@crowncreative.co.uk  www.crowncreative.co.uk

Printed in the UK by John Price Printers Limited. Tel: 01902 353 441  www.john-price.co.uk

No images may be reproduced without the prior permission of the individual copyright holders and the publishers.

# Contents

# Arthur Wharton

When Arthur Wharton signed for Rotherham Town in 1889 he became the world's first black professional footballer almost a century before the pioneering impact made by Cyrille Regis, Brendon Batson and Laurie Cunningham at West Bromwich Albion.

Arthur Wharton was an extraordinary man in many ways. The son of mixed race parents, his father a Methodist minister, he arrived in England as a teenager in 1865 from Africa's Gold Coast, now Ghana, to train to become a missionary.

His athletic prowess soon became apparent and by 1886 he had become the fastest man in Britain, breaking the national 100 yard sprint record at Stamford Bridge as well as setting the record time for cycling between Preston and Blackburn.

It was, however, football that was his first love and, in particular, the position of goalkeeper. Modern followers of the game might wonder why the fastest man in Britain would choose to play in goal but this was a time when the goalkeeper was still allowed to handle the ball anywhere in his own half and could be charged down by opposition players whether he had the ball or not. He needed to be fast, agile – and very tough.

In 1886 Arthur joined Preston North End - 'the Invincibles' - as an amateur and the following year played in goal against West Bromwich Albion in the FA Cup semi-final.

## *'Arthur Wharton signed for Rotherham Town in 1889 to become the world's first black professional footballer'*

Three years later, in 1889, he took what we now see as the historic step of signing professional papers for Rotherham Town where he also took over the management of the local pub, The Plough Inn, and married local girl, Emma Lister.

In 1894 he signed for Sheffield United where he made his first division debut and became the first black player in the top flight of the Football League before returning to Rotherham the following year who had since changed their name from Town to United.

Never one to settle, he finished his football career playing for a string of clubs across Lancashire before returning to play professional cricket in the Yorkshire Leagues until well into his fifties.

### Arthur Wharton

**Clubs:**
Preston North End, Rotherham Town, Sheffield Utd, Rotherham Utd, Stalybridge Athletic, Ashton North End, Stockport County.

Arthur Wharton became a true working class hero during his lifetime and was extremely well respected in the communities within which he lived and played his sport. He was, undoubtedly, the victim of racism but he was also a proud man and fought back to become a standard bearer for the generations of black footballers who would go on to shape the game nearly a century later.

# Walter Tull

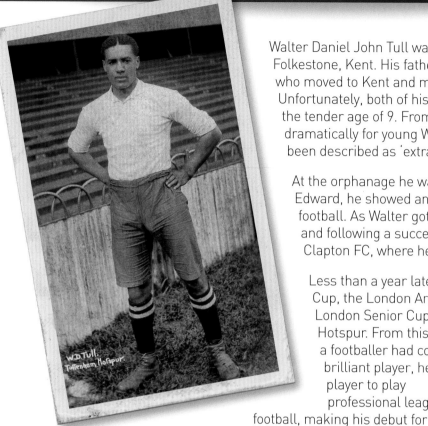

W.D. Tull.
Tottenham Hotspur.

Walter Daniel John Tull was born on 28th April 1888 in Folkestone, Kent. His father was a Barbadian carpenter, who moved to Kent and married the love of his life. Unfortunately, both of his parents died when Tull was at the tender age of 9. From that point on things changed dramatically for young Walter and his life story has often been described as 'extraordinary'.

At the orphanage he was taken in to with his brother Edward, he showed an exceptional talent for the sport of football. As Walter got older, his love for football grew and following a successful trial he was signed by Clapton FC, where he played inside-forward.

Less than a year later, after winning the FA Amateur Cup, the London Amateur County Cup AND the London Senior Cup, he was noticed by Tottenham Hotspur. From this moment on, his dream of being a footballer had come true. But, not only was he a brilliant player, he was also the first black outfield player to play professional league football, making his debut for Tottenham in September 1909 against Sunderland. Tull transferred to Northampton Town in 1911 where he managed 111 first team appearances for the club.

## 'The first black outfield player to play professional league football'

Despite the racial taunts and abuse, he was still described by a journalist at the Spurs v Bristol City match in 1909 as a 'model for all white men who play football'

During the First World War, Tull served in the Middlesex Regiment and fought at the Battle of the Somme in 1916. He was commissioned a Second Lieutenant on 30th May 1917 despite the 1914 Manual of Military Law preventing "Negroes" from exercising command as Officers. Tull was commended for his gallantry and coolness whilst fighting in Italy leading 26 men on a raiding party in enemy territory.

Tull was killed in action on 25th March 1918.

WALTER TULL
FOOTBALL

The Greater Game
Sport, War and Peace
IMPERIAL | WAR MUSEUM | NORTH

ENGLAND, TOTTENHAM HOTSPUR AND NORTHAMPTON TOWN

### Walter Tull

**Clubs:**
Clapton FC, Tottenham Hotspur, Northampton Town.

# John Edward Parris

John Edward Parris, also known as Eddie or Ted Parris was born in Wales on 31st January 1911. He was the first black football player to represent Wales in an international. He played for Bradford Park Avenue, AFC Bournemouth, Luton Town, Bath City, Northampton Town and Cheltenham Town.

He played for Chepstow Town F.C. before he was noticed by scouts for Bradford Park Avenue F.C. a leading club at the time who signed him as a trialist in 1928. He made his debut in January 1929, scoring his team's only goal in a drawn FA Cup match against Hull. After this he established a regular first-team place at left wing. In his career at Bradford Park Avenue, he played 142 League and Cup games and scored 39 goals.

In December 1931 Parris made his first and only appearance for Wales against Ireland in Belfast, becoming the first black player to represent Wales in an international. Although sometimes cited as the first black player to play for any of the 'home countries', research says that in fact the first was the Scotland player Andrew Watson.

## *'The first black player to represent Wales in an international'*

*Ted Parris*

Parris suffered an injury in 1934 but went on to play for Bournemouth (1934–37), Luton, Northampton, Bath City, Cheltenham Town and Gloucester City. He later worked in an airplane factory and died in Gloucestershire, England in 1971.

### John Edward Parris

**Clubs:**
Chepstow FC, Bradford Park Avenue, AFC Bournemouth, Luton Town, Bath City, Northampton Town, Cheltenham Town.

**International Caps:** 1

# Lindy Delaphena

Lindy Delaphena was born in Jamaica on 25th May 1927 and served with the British armed forces in the Middle East following World War II.

In 1947 an English football scout saw him playing football for the British Army and recommended him to Arsenal who gave him a trial as an amateur but did not sign him as a professional player.

**PORTSMOUTH 1948/49**
Back Row: Rookes, Foxton, Hudson, Reid, Juliussen, Humpston, Butler, Field, Flewin, Bowler, Thompson, Neave.
Middle Row: D.Clarke (Sec), R.Lever (Asst.Mgr), Evans, Asher, Beale, Drummond, Elder, Yeuell, Spence, Dickinson, Ferrier, Delapenha, J.Easson (Asst.Trn), J.Stewart (Trn).
Front Row: Froggatt, Scoular, Phillips, Brown, Newman, Barlow, R.Jackson (Mgr), Parker, McDonald, Lawler, Harris, Clarke, Hindmarr

MIDDLESBROUGH F.C. 1952-53
LEFT TO RIGHT - BACK ROW :- H.SHEPHERDSON (Trainer), RUSSELL, ROBINSON, UGOLINI, DELAPENHA, CORBETT, DICKS.
FRONT ROW :- MOCHAN, MANNION, BELL, WHITAKER, FITZSIMMONS, WALKER.

His luck changed the following year when he joined Portsmouth and played seven games during their 1948-9 League Championship winning season to become the first black player to win a League Championship medal.

After two successful years with Portsmouth, Lindy transferred to Middlesbrough in April 1950 where his career moved into gear and he became a great favourite with the Ayresome Park crowd.

## 'The first black player to win a League Championship medal in 1948-49'

Playing on the wing or at inside-forward, Lindy became Boro's leading scorer in the 1951-52, 1953-54 and 1955-56 seasons. In total he scored 93 league and FA Cup goals in 270 appearances.

He moved to Mansfield Town in June 1958, scoring 27 goals in 115 appearances over a period of two years, before retiring from League football in 1960.

### Lindy Delaphena

**Clubs:**
Portsmouth, Middlesbrough, Mansfield Town.

# Henry Roy Brown

Henry Brown was the son of a Nigerian father and English mother. Stoke was his home town and the place where he grew up playing football. Brown joined Stoke City in 1939, but the football league was interrupted by World War II and he joined up to serve with the British Army during the war.

The Football League did not reform until the 1946 season. Brown made history in that first season by playing in Stoke's 3-1 win over Preston North End; he was the first black player to play for Stoke City. Although he was a talented player, he played sporadically in the first team, often as a substitute until he started to get regular appearances in the 1950-51 season when he played 29 games.

Brown was keen to get more regular play and so he left Stoke City for Third Division side Watford. His first season there saw him score 21 goals. He remained at Watford for four more seasons before seeing out his career with non-league Chelmsford City.

Brown was a determined footballer fighting against early prejudice to continue doing what he loved. He was a patriot and a a true lover of the game.

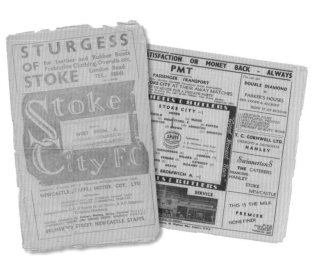

*'The first black player to play for Stoke City'*

**Henry Roy Brown**

**Clubs:**
Stoke City, Watford FC, Chelmsford City.

# Charlie Williams

Charlie Williams was born on 23rd December 1928 in Royston, South Yorkshire, a small mining village near Barnsley. His father, also Charles, had come to England in 1914 from Barbados, and enlisted in the Royal Engineers.

After the First World War, his father settled in Royston, where he sold groceries from a horse and cart and married a local girl, Frances Cook.

After leaving school aged 14, Williams worked at Upton Colliery during the Second World War, a reserved occupation. He played football for the colliery team before turning professional and signing for Doncaster Rovers in 1948.

Charlie became one of the first black players in the Football League and between 1955 and 1959 he was the regular centre-half for Doncaster Rovers appearing in 157 league games and scoring one goal.

Derek Kevan (WBA) and Charlie Williams watch as Doncaster Rovers goalkeeper Harry Gregg turns the ball past the post.

During this time Charlie was self deprecating about his own footballing ability and he was often quoted as saying "I was never a fancy player, but I could stop them buggers that were."

He ended his football career with Skegness Town in the Midland League and entered the world of show business.

He became a key part of 'The Comedians' TV show, which was notorious for promoting racial stereotypes, and deflated what some of those comedians were doing by the sheer power of his personality. He was known for his catchphrase "me old flower", which was delivered in a broad Yorkshire accent, and his put-down to hecklers, "If you don't shut up, I'll come and move in next door to you."

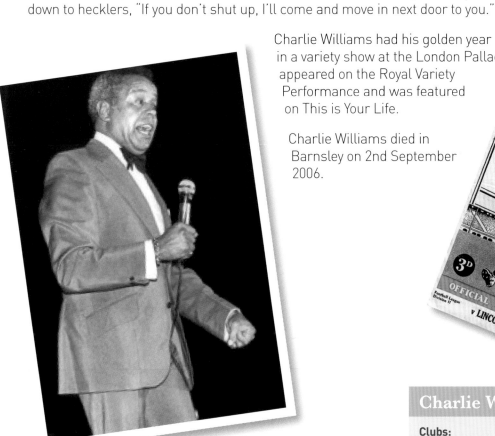

Charlie Williams had his golden year in 1972. He starred in a variety show at the London Palladium for six months, appeared on the Royal Variety Performance and was featured on This is Your Life.

Charlie Williams died in Barnsley on 2nd September 2006.

## Charlie Williams

**Clubs:**
Doncaster Rovers, Skegness Town.

# Albert Johanneson

Some people believed that a black footballer playing in the final of the world's foremost club competition in 1960's England was, in a sporting context, as extraordinary as Barack Obama being made the first black president of the U.S. In the immediate years before, no one realistically could have expected or even predicted either occurrence. After all, Albert Johanneson was a man who before his arrival on British shores, normally ran without footwear and even played soccer without boots.

Albert had to suffer so much over-the-top treatment from people he had never even met before, people who possessed no idea of what he was like as a person but who inexplicably regarded him as an enemy. Over-the-top treatment on and off the field of play often occurred, sometimes in the form of crude attempts at humour, often in the form of real malice. But this isn't the place to focus on that, this is a reminder, a celebration of sorts of what Albert accomplished following his 1961 arrival in the grim Northern terrain of South Leeds, culminating in his Cup Final appearance for the all-whites of Leeds United versus the all-reds of Liverpool.

It wasn't just his colour that made Albert Johanneson stand out, nor was it the rarely seen contrast of his team's white strip against his black skin. No, he helped light up English football by virtue of his ability. He was fast, very fast, he was tricky and he was skilful, very skilful. The ball was his friend, it stuck with him, virtually always in his control as if supernaturally magnetised to his feet. To see him speeding towards bewildered and worried back-pedalling full-backs was a scintillating sight most fans had rarely witnessed before. English club football was tough in those days, even tougher in Division Two where Albert commenced his Leeds career, the club toiling in the lower reaches of that second tier. He gradually toughened up after coming here from South Africa, and he was in the best physical condition he had ever been in thanks to the training regime at Elland Road. He also learned to tolerate, to a certain extent, opponents' fouls and frequent bodily assaults on him which usually went unpunished by referees. At times though, the injuries inflicted on him did take their toll, as he was forced to miss matches in each of his seasons at Leeds.

WITH THE COMPLIMENTS OF Ty·Phoo TEA LTD., BIRMINGHAM 5

LEEDS UNITED F.C.
Back row, L to R: Hair, Reaney, Sprake, Charlton, Bell, Hunter
Front row, L to R: Henderson, Johanneson, Storrie, Collins, Bremner

Small in stature, big in talent, a quiet and sensitive man, Albert brought much-needed creativity, potency and pace to a gravely lacking Leeds side. On the wing ('outside-left' in those days) he supplied the Leeds attack with elements they had so often missed: flair and service. He was in those early days the only glamour in a drab team more used to a pressing, hard running style of play typical of that division, and a team too used to not winning.

Albert played his first game in April 1961. New manager Don Revie had promised Leeds fans that Albert would excite them. He wasn't wrong, it took Albert quite some time to play consistently well but nonetheless, he was often good, occasionally brilliant, and naturally always a main attraction. He was not the first black Leeds player, or indeed the first South African to appear for the club. That honour belongs to Gerry Francis but Albert Johanneson possessed much more in his footballing armoury. And Gerry was certainly no slouch. The Leeds supporters quickly gave Albert nicknames, like The Black Flash, A.J., Hurry Hurry or even Go-Go Jo-Jo. There were uncorroborated stories of a few Leeds fans throwing bananas on to the Elland Road pitch, with him and a few of the other players eating them before kick-off, but the welcome generally given by the people of Leeds was extremely affectionate and supportive. Ignorance is no excuse of course but it is hard to believe that personal offence had been intended.

## 'The first black player to appear in a FA Cup Final'

In 1965, Leeds had enjoyed a rare run of success in the FA Cup. After beating Southport in the 3rd round, they went on to knock out Everton, Shrewsbury Town and Crystal Palace before meeting arch rivals Manchester United in the semi-final. After a 0-0 draw, the replay saw a Leeds victory, Billy Bremner scoring a spectacular diving header in the closing moments. Albert however, had been ruled out of the replay as a result of the 'Nobby Stiles effect' in the first game! The final would be against Liverpool. It would be Leeds United's Wembley debut.

Alas, Albert had an awful game against Liverpool. He wasn't injured, at least not physically. People said he 'froze', overawed by the occasion, but there was more to it than that. You see, whenever he got the ball, hundreds, possibly thousands, of Liverpool fans booed, jeered and whistled him. Quite trivial however compared to their grunting, screeching and monkey noises aimed at him. The poor fella never got a moment's peace and he 'shrank' throughout the match as a result.

From 1961, Albert may have toughened up physically, but mentally, emotionally, he remained vulnerable, the insults and jibes always hurt him deeply. Despite his popularity and his successes, he lacked confidence and suffered from loneliness too. A quote from his good pal Billy Bremner - '... it was as if Albert couldn't believe it was happening to him, as if he thought a black man wasn't entitled to be famous'.

**Albert Johanneson**

**Clubs:**
Leeds Utd, York City.

# Mike Trebilcock

Mike Trebilcock was the 21-year-old star of Everton's 1966 FA Cup triumph. He scored twice in six second-half minutes as the Merseysiders beat Sheffield Wednesday 3-2 in the final at Wembley. This memorable achievement came out of the blue after his boss at Goodison Park, Harry Catterick, had chosen him ahead of England international centre-forward Fred Pickering, despite Trebilcock having been out of action for four months and well short of match practice.

Everton were 2-0 down before the Cornish forward said 'thank you' by producing what transpired to be a match-winning performance.

Signed initially as a professional by Plymouth Argyle boss Malcolm Allison from Tavistock, Trebilcock made his Football League debut in a 1-0 Second Division win over Swansea Town at Home Park in November 1962. He went on to net 29 goals in 81 games for the Pilgrims before joining Everton for £23,000 on New Year's Eve in 1965.

He subsequently made his first appearance in the top flight of English football, helping Everton draw 2-2 with Tottenham Hotspur at White Hart Lane 24 hours later. He then scored his first goal for his new club in a 2-0 home win over Aston Villa a week later. Unable to hold down a regular place in the team, Trebilcock netted only five goals for Everton in a total of 15 first-class appearances before transferring to Portsmouth in January 1968 for a club record fee of £40,000. He went on to average a goal every three games for Pompey (36 in 121 games) before winding down his senior career by scoring 11 times in 26 appearances for Torquay. After a short spell in non-League football with Weymouth, Trebilcock emigrated to Sydney, Australia where he played for and later managed Western Suburbs FC, winning the NSW Rothman's medal in 1974.

## Mike Trebilcock

**Clubs:**
Plymouth Argyle, Everton, Portsmouth, Torquay, Western Suburbs FC (Aus).

# Clyde Best

Clyde Best was a true black football pioneer.

After playing for Ireland Rangers and Somerset Trojans Club in Bermuda he travelled to London in in 1968 to sign for West Ham United.

This was the time when television was providing football with an opportunity to market the game to a new audience in the euphoric years that followed England winning the World Cup in 1966.

Bobby Moore, Martin Peters and Geoff Hurst became national heroes and Clyde Best lined up alongside these players for West Ham United following his debut in a 1-1 home draw against Arsenal on 25 August 1969.

Best developed into a fast powerful centre forward who was seen as the Black Roy of the Rovers by young black men who saw him play both on the pitch and on television.

He inspired these youngsters to believe that if they worked hard enough black men could succeed as professional footballers.

Like his great friend Cyrille Regis at West Bromwich Albion, Best was often the subject of mindless racist taunts but he used this abuse as motivation and found the most effective response was to stick the ball in the back of the net.

In spite of his fame Clyde Best never came over as the big time football star, he was, and remains to this day a very warm and genuine man who made an enormous contribution to the fight for racial equality in football.

He laid to rest the myth that black players could not play in cold weather, had weak ankles and were afraid of the physical side of the game.

Best did this by playing 186 games for West Ham and scoring 47 goals seasons between August 1969 and January 1976.

During this time he helped to remove some of the racial barriers in professional football and helped the black players of today to become such an important and integral part of our national game.

## Clyde Best

**Clubs:**
West Ham Utd, Feyenoord,
Tampa Bay Rowdies (USA),
Toronto Blizzard (CAN),
Portland Timbers (USA).

# Ces Podd

**CES PODD**
Bradford City

Cyril Casey Marcel 'Ces' Podd arrived from the Caribbean in 1961 to Britain when he was nine years old. Podd immediately set about to get himself noticed in football by playing regularly for his school, church and youth club. He thought the more clubs he played for the better his chances would be of getting spotted by a talent scout.

Podd's early attempts to break into football got off to a false start when he applied for trials at Manchester United and Wolverhampton Wanderers but didn't even get to play due to the fact that he was black. Ces decided enough was enough and set off for Art College in Bradford. However, he couldn't resist when another opportunity for a trial came his way at Bradford City. He was asked to play left wing (when his usual position was right back) and was so keen to make an impression that he accepted the position even though it meant the challenge of learning to play with his left foot!

Podd made a name for himself in 1971 against Chesterfield and was named Man of the Match in the local press. After being seen in the newspaper Ces received a lot of racial abuse. Name calling, spitting and having bananas thrown at him was part and parcel of the terraces in the 1970's and 80's.

However, Podd fought against the racism and became a regular fixture at Bradford City making 565 appearances over the next 14 seasons.

In 1980 Podd was the first black footballer to be granted a testimonial by the Football Association. In his team were names such as Garth Crooks, Luther Blissett, Alex Williams, Vince Hilaire, Terry Connor, Justin Fashanu and Cyrille Regis. Podd was a trailblazer for young black players and he used his testimonial as the opportunity to bring together a new generation of young black players who had followed in his footsteps.

*'The first black footballer to be granted a testimonial by the FA'*

## Ces Podd

**Clubs:**
Bradford City, Halifax Town, Scarborough Town.

# Tony Ford

Tony Ford was born in Grimsby on 14th May 1959. He joined his hometown club in 1975 and made his debut for the Mariners as a substitute in a 3rd Division game at Walsall on 4th October 1975. Following another appearance as a sub at Brighton he made his full debut at Swindon Town on 25th October. At 16 years and 164 days he was the youngest player to make his full debut for Grimsby. It was the start of a playing career that would span 26 years during which he would play 931 league games for nine clubs. This would constitute a record for an outfield player and only the great Peter Shilton has played more league games than Tony.

Initially Tony spent 11 years at Blundell Park where he was voted Supporters Club Young Player of The Year in 1976, won a 3rd Division Championship Medal in 1980 and was voted Supporters Club Player of The Year in 1984 and 1985. In 1986 following a short loan period at Sunderland he left his boyhood club joining Stoke City on a permanent deal. Ford spent two and a half years with the Potters before signing for West Bromwich Albion in March 1989 where he teamed up with his old Stoke colleague Brian Talbot who was player manager for the Baggies. Ford, who could operate at right back or on the right wing, made an immediate impact at The Hawthorns so much so that at the end of the season he was chosen to play for the England "B" team on their three game tour of Europe. Tony gained three caps appearing as a substitute against Switzerland and Iceland and a full game against Norway.

## 'The first black player to complete over 1000 games in English football'

Ford returned "home" to Grimsby in November 1991. His stay was brief and a loan move to Bradford City followed before he moved to Scunthorpe United in 1994. He left league football for a short sojourn at Barrow in 1996. From there it was on to Mansfield Town where his former Stoke team mate Steve Parkin was in charge. At Field Mill in early 1999 he played his 825th League game against Plymouth Argyle. This broke the previous record held by Terry Paine (Southampton and Hereford) for the record number of appearances for an outfield player. To recognise this feat he was awarded the PFA Merit award in 1999.

All told Tony played in 1080 League and Cup games in his career scoring 125 goals. That figure is testimony to his professionalism, fitness, dedication and aptitude in a game which he clearly loved. No black player has played more games than Tony Ford and only one other outfield player, Graham Alexander, has passed 1000 competitive (League and Cup) matches in English football.

### Tony Ford

**Clubs:**
Grimsby Town, Stoke City, West Bromwich Albion, Bradford City, Scunthorpe United, Mansfield Town, Rochdale.

# Viv Anderson

Viv Anderson holds a special place in the history of black players in English football. On 29th November 1978 he became the first black player to represent England in a full International when he appeared against Czechoslovakia at Wembley. It was the culmination of a rapid rise to fame which had begun six years earlier in the Second Division with Nottingham Forest.

Vivian Alexander Anderson was born in Nottingham on 29th August 1956. He played for Nottingham Schoolboys and when he left school he became an apprentice printer. In 1972 he joined Nottingham Forest as an apprentice pro and quickly established himself in their youth and reserve sides. At 6'2" he had a long stride and with his gangly legs he acquired the nickname "spider". In 1974 he signed his first contract as a professional, making his league debut for Forest in the Second Division on 21st September 1974 in a 3-2 win at Sheffield Wednesday. In 1976/77 Viv helped Forest gain promotion to Division One, a triumph which heralded a golden age for Forest and Viv's rise to stardom.

Under Brian Clough Forest took the football world by storm and in 1977/78 Anderson played in 50 League and Cup games as the East Midlands club carried off the First Division Championship and the League Cup. The following season Anderson and Forest scaled new heights. Viv gained his first England cap and then went on to win a European Cup winners medal when the reds defeated Malmö 1-0 in the Final on 30th May 1979.

At international level his appearances were limited, mainly because of the fierce competition from the established old boys such as Phil Neal and Mick Mills. Nevertheless Anderson's career continued to blossom and whilst at the City Ground he added another European Cup medal in 1980 and 7 England "B" Caps to his trophy cabinet. For the next four years he was Forest's established right back, where his height proved invaluable at both defensive and attacking set pieces resulting in 22 league and Cup goals in his time at Forest.

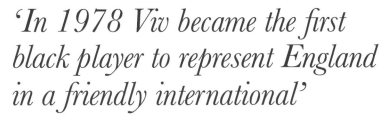

## 'In 1978 Viv became the first black player to represent England in a friendly international'

In 1984 he moved to Arsenal for a fee of £250,000. In his three years at Highbury he became an attacking full back scoring 15 goals in 150 games for the Gunners. Anderson travelled to Mexico with the England party for the 1986 World Cup Finals but he did not play a game. By way of consolation he won another League Cup winners medal in 1987 as Arsenal beat Liverpool 2-1 in the final. After three short years in London Viv was on the move again leaving the marbled halls of Highbury for the theatre of dreams in Manchester.

Anderson signed for Manchester United in the summer of 1987 in an acrimonious move which saw the fee of £250,000 decided by an independent tribunal. His time at Old Trafford was plagued by injuries, as the Red Devils finished as League runners up. His experience and ability were seen as invaluable assets to the emerging youngsters in Alex Ferguson's side. The boys that Anderson cajoled and encouraged were to become the bedrock of the United team that would eventually sweep all before them. In 1988 Anderson won the last of his 30 England caps when he played against Columbia at Wembley. Injuries and the emergence of Lee Martin at Old Trafford finally took their toll resulting in a free transfer to Sheffield Wednesday in January 1991.

At the age of 31 Anderson embarked on the twilight of his career. At Hillsborough he shook off the injuries that had plagued him in Manchester and as captain of the Owls he led them to promotion in his first season in Sheffield and in 1993 he was leader of the side who reached the FA Cup and League Cup Finals, losing both to his old club Arsenal. At the end of 1992/93 he switched to Barnsley as player manager but his sojourn there was brief and after one season he linked up with his old Manchester United team mate Bryan Robson at Middlesbrough where he became assistant manager to "captain marvel." The pair gained promotion to the Premier League twice and got to three cup finals, sadly losing all three. In 2001 Steve McClaren took over in Teesside and Viv left the club to end his association with the coaching side of the game.

Viv Anderson's place in football history is assured, when he left the game he still continued to be involved through the media and charity work. For a time he was Patron for Youth Against Racism and in the Millennium Honours List he received an MBE from the Queen for his services to Football. A fitting tribute to the man who created history.

### Viv Anderson

**Clubs:**
Nottingham Forest, Arsenal, Man Utd, Sheffield Wednesday, Barnsley, Middlesbrough.

**England Caps:** 30

# Garth Crooks

Garth Crooks was the proverbial local boy made good, raised within a stone's throw of the Victoria Ground in Stoke, he was to forge a fine career as a footballer and make his own little bit of history too.

Garth Anthony Crooks was born in Stoke on Trent on 10th March 1958. He was a product of St Peters Comprehensive School, joining Stoke City as an apprentice in 1974. Garth, coached by Gordon Banks, graduated through the Potters youth set up making his full league debut for Stoke at Coventry on 10th April 1976 in a 1-0 reverse. In his first season for Stoke in 1976/77, he was top scorer with 6 goals but the Potters were relegated. The following term Crooks netted 18 times to finish as leading marksman again.

In 1978/79 under Alan Durban the Potters were promoted and in November 1979 he made his debut for the England Under 21 side at Filbert Street, Leicester, against Bulgaria. Garth scored a hat trick in a 5-0 win thus becoming the first black player to net three goals in an England shirt. At the end of the 1979/80 season, following a disagreement with Alan Durban Crooks moved to Spurs for a fee of £650,000.

## 'The first black player to score a hat-trick in an England shirt'

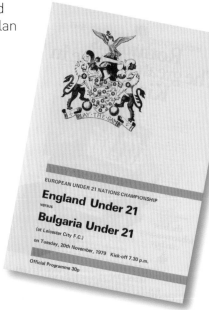

EUROPEAN UNDER 21 NATIONS CHAMPIONSHIP

**England Under 21**
versus
**Bulgaria Under 21**
(at Leicester City F.C.)

on Tuesday, 20th November, 1979  Kick-off 7.30 p.m.

Official Programme 30p

At Tottenham Garth played alongside Ossie Ardiles, Ricky Villa and his strike partner Steve Archibald. In 1980/81 Spurs reached the FA Cup final against Manchester City, drawing 1-1. In the replay at Wembley, City took the lead but just as the Blues seemed to be taking control Crooks equalised for Tottenham who went on to win 3-2.

In 1981/82, Spurs and Crooks retained the old trophy defeating QPR 1-0 in another replay. They also reached the League Cup Final where they were beaten by Liverpool.

In 1982/83, Garth found himself out of the Spurs side and in 1983/84 he had a brief spell on loan to Manchester United. When Spurs signed Clive Allen in 1984 the writing was on the wall for the man from Stoke and in August 1985 he joined West Bromwich Albion for £100,000.

In his initial season at the Hawthorns Garth served three managers, John Giles, Nobby Stiles and Ron Saunders as Albion were relegated to Division Two. Saunders and Crooks never saw eye to eye and in the great Baggies clear out of March 1987 Garth was transferred to Charlton, where due to an ongoing back problem his career ended in May 1990. At the time he was Chairman of the PFA having been elected to the post in 1988. In October 1999 Garth was awarded the OBE for services to The Institute of Professional Sport. He now enjoys a successful career as a media pundit.

### Garth Crooks

**Clubs:**
Stoke City, Tottenham Hotspur, Man Utd, West Bromwich Albion, Charlton Athletic.

# Ricky Hill

Bobby Robson took over as England manager in the autumn of 1982. His first match in charge was a game against Denmark in Copenhagen on 22nd September 1982, a European Championship Qualifier. England drew 2-2 and Robson selected one new cap in his team, Ricky Hill of Luton Town. Hill was only the fourth black player to play for the full England team and he was also the first black player that Robson selected in his tenure as the manager of the national side. Ricky came on as a second half substitute replacing Bryan Robson. He went on to win three caps.

Ricky Anthony Hill was born in Paddington on 3rd March 1959. In a long and fruitful career he played for Luton Town for fourteen years becoming one of their greatest ever footballers. Hill signed for the Hatters in 1975, he was spotted by their reserve team coach David Pleat whilst playing for John Kelly Boys Technology College in Neasden. He made his league debut as a seventeen-year-old substitute at Kenilworth Road scoring in a 3-1 win over Bristol City.

Ricky quickly became a first team regular and in 1981-82 he was part of the Hatters line up that won the Second Division Championship. His silky midfield skills and close ball control made him a firm favourite with the Luton fans and his early season form in 1982 earned him his England call up. His consistent performances and the astute management of Pleat helped Luton to the most successful period in their history. In 1985 Luton reached the FA Cup semi final. Hill scored but they lost to Everton 2-1 after extra time at Villa Park. Undeterred the Luton bandwagon marched on and in 1988 Luton reached Wembley where they defeated Arsenal 3-2 in the League Cup Final. Hill was a star as the Hatters won their first major trophy. In the same season they were FA Cup semi finalists again, losing to Wimbledon at White Hart Lane.

In 1989 after his sterling service at Kenilworth Road Ricky was granted a free transfer, hopping over the Channel to join the French side Le Havre. It turned out to be a brief sojourn and before long in August 1990 he returned to England, teaming up with his old boss David Pleat at Leicester City. In his solitary season at Filbert Street he helped the Foxes avoid relegation to the Third Division. Hill then left the East Midlands for America joining Tampa Bay Rowdies. As their coach he led them to two National Championships and in 1992 he was awarded the accolade of "Coach of the Year."

After short spells at Chertsey Hitchin, Luton and Spurs (as youth team coach) he had an unsuccessful stint as manager at Luton in 2000 before returning to the USA where he won the Soccer Super Bowl as coach of Tampa Bay in 2012.

**Ricky Hill**

**Clubs:**
Luton Town, Le Havre, Leicester City, Tampa Bay Rowdies.

**England Caps:** 3

# Luther Blissett

Luther Blissett is a Watford legend who had three spells at Vicarage Road and has made more appearances and scored more goals than any other player in their history. He played fourteen times for England scoring three goals, all of them in one game which gives a unique place in the annals of the national side. He was the first black player to score a hat trick in a full England international.

Born in Falmouth, Jamaica on 1st February 1958. Luther moved to England with his family at a very early age. He grew up in Willesden and signed for Watford as an apprentice in 1974, turning professional in 1975. Luther made his first team debut as a substitute in a Fourth Division game against Barnsley on 3rd April 1976. Watford won 1-0. In 1977-78 Graham Taylor was appointed as the Watford manager. He was impressed with Blissett and made him a first team regular. The tall rangy striker became the fulcrum of the Hornets attack. Watford were promoted to Division Three in 1978 and the next year they went up to Division Two and Luther was voted into the PFA Third Division Team of the season. With Blissett and Ross Jenkins as a deadly strike force Watford won promotion to the First Division in 1981-82 for the first time in their history.

## 'The first black player to score a hat trick in a full England international'

For his sterling efforts Luther was rewarded with an England call up in October 1982. He had already turned out for the B team and the U21 side but on 31st October 1982 he gained his first full cap when he played against West Germany at Wembley as a second half substitute. Two months later on 15th December he had his first start as England played Luxembourg in a European Championship Qualifier at Wembley. England won 9-0, Blissett scored a hat trick, the first one by a black player for the full England side and although he never scored again for England Luther had claimed his place in the history of the national team.

Watford finished runners up in the First Division in 1982-83. In scoring twenty seven league goals Blissett was the leading league goalscorer in Europe and was awarded 'The Golden Boot' for his achievement. In June 1983 A.C. Milan paid £1 million for his services but his time in Italy was short, unhappy and unsuccessful, so much so that he moved back to Vicarage Road for £50,000 in the summer of 1984.

His second spell at Watford was less rewarding. The Hornets began a slow decline which saw them relegated back to the second tier in 1988. Luther moved on to Bournemouth where in a three year period he netted a goal every other game to continue a remarkable scoring record. In 1991 he went back to Watford for the third and final time as a player. Further moves to West Brom (loan) Derry City (loan), Bury and Mansfield followed, ending his professional career at Field Mill on the 18th January 1994 scoring in a 2-1 victory over Hereford.

He had short spells at Southport, Wimbourne, Fakenham Town and Chesham (as manager) before joining Watford again in 1996 as a coach until 2001.

Since leaving football Luther has worked in the media and also in motorsport, a passion he shares with Les Ferdinand and John Barnes enabling him to raise money for The Bobby Moore Cancer Trust and Prostate Cancer research.

Brendon Batson, Cyrille Regis and Luther Blissett show the Civil Rights Leader Martin Luther King III, the Laurie Cunningham Trophy at the Kick it Out 20th Anniversary Dinner at Wembley Stadium.

**Luther Blissett**

**Clubs:**
Watford, AC Milan, Bournemouth, West Bromwich Albion, Derry City, Bury, Mansfield.

**England Caps:** 14

# George Berry

Born in Germany on 19th November 1957, Berry became known as a tough tackler in defence throughout his professional career. The Berry family moved to Blackpool soon after George's birth and his football career began. He started playing football at school and local youth club and was recommended for a trial at Wolverhampton Wanderers. Berry was determined that football was the career for him and the day after he finished his 'O' levels at school, he signed a contract with Wolves. He turned professional on his 18th birthday and made his debut against Chelsea on 7th May 1977.

Berry was a popular player amongst many of the fans, winning player of the year in 1979 and helping Wolves to win the 1980 League Cup.

It wasn't all smooth sailing for Berry; he encountered racism even from Wolves supporters. He was very angry at the time with the racist abuse from the terraces especially from the home fans.

On Wolves finding themselves relegated in the 1981/82 season, Berry left and signed for Stoke City. At Stoke Berry was well received showing great determination and commitment to the game. However, he found himself demoted to the youth team when new manager Bill Asprey took over at Stoke in 1983. Berry did return to the first team in the 1984/85 season but it was a record low for Stoke who finished the season with only 17 points. Berry soon found himself back on form and captained the team in the 1986/87 season. All in all he made 267 appearances for Stoke City and scored 29 goals.

Berry enjoyed a brief international career for his mother's native Wales. He was capped five times before he retired in the mid-1990s.

Since retiring from professional football, Berry has demonstrated his head for business by gaining a degree and taking up the post of Commercial Executive at Stafford Rangers before becoming a Senior Commercial Executive for the PFA where he works today.

GEORGE BERRY

RobBond 2005

## George Berry

**Clubs:**
Wolverhampton Wanderers, Stoke City, Doncaster Rovers, Peterborough Utd, Preston North End.

**Wales Caps:** 5

# Brian Stein

Luton Town manager David Pleat signed striker Brian Stein in 1977. This was the first of two spells with the Kenilworth Road club for whom he made 427 League appearances and scored 130 goals.

Initially a winger, he formed prolific partnerships with Bob Hatton and Steve White as the Hatters won the Second Division title in 1981-82 and the following season, with Paul Walsh his co-striker. Luton started with a flurry of bravura attacking performances in the early weeks of the season, including 5-0 and 5-3 home victories over Brighton and Notts County and 4-4 and 3-3 draws at Stoke and Liverpool respectively. Unfortunately, that initial excitement and promise faded as Luton struggled, not least because Stein was sidelined with a broken foot from December onwards.

Luton needed to win their last game of the season at Manchester City to avoid relegation and send City down instead. Stein returned to the team, despite lacking match fitness, and helped set up Raddy Antic's dramatic winner four minutes from time. An excited David Pleat then gambolled across the pitch at the final whistle to hug his players.

Stein's finest hour, however, as a Luton player came on 24th April 1988 when he scored twice, including the late winner, in Luton's 3–2 League Cup final victory over Arsenal at Wembley.

Stein joined the French club Stade Malherbe de Caen in 1989 and a year later signed for Annecy, before rejoining Luton in 1991. Unfortunately this time the Hatters were relegated at the end of the season, ending a run of ten successive seasons of top flight football, all but three of which Stein was an integral part of.

He signed for Barnet in 1992 and retired in May 1993, having scored 204 goals in 624 club matches, as well as gaining one full cap (in a 2-0 defeat by France in Paris in 1984) and three U21 caps for England, helping them win the European Championship at this level.

Stein's brother, Mark, also played for Luton Town as well as QPR, Chelsea and Stoke City, among others.

## Brian Stein

**Clubs:**
Luton Town, Stade Malherbe de Caen, Annecy, Barnet.

**England Caps:** 1

# Ruud Gullit

Ruud Gullit honed his early football skills playing street football with other boys near to his home before joining the DWS club at the age of 10. He soon came to the attention of scouts for the Dutch youth team and began playing regularly for the national youth side. Gullit made his international debut for the Dutch team at the age of 19 and helped them win at Euro 1988 and qualify for the 1990 World Cup.

Gullit signed for his first professional club HFC Haarlem in 1978 under former West Bromwich Albion player Barry Hughes. He made 91 league appearances and scored 32 goals for the team. Gullit was just 16 at the time of his professional debut making him the youngest player (at the time) in the history of the Eredivisie.

Gullit was considered for a transfer by Arsenal and Ipswich Town, but finally moved to Feyenoord in 1982. He made 85 league appearances and scored 31 goals and helped Feyenoord to league and cup double in 1983. Gullit was named Dutch player of the year in recognition of his contribution to the club's success. He sadly encountered racism whilst at Feyenoord, including abuse from manager Thijs Libregts who referred to Gullit as 'blackie' and criticised him for being lazy. Gullit also encountered racism from Scottish fans when Feyenoord played St Mirren in September 1983. He was subject to verbal abuse and spitting and referred to the events as "the saddest night of my life".

Despite suffering racist abuse, Gullit's career went from strength to strength when he joined PSV Eindhoven in 1985 and scored 46 goals in 68 league appearances. He was again named Dutch player of the Year in 1986.

Gullit soon moved on to AC Milan in 1987 and enjoyed domestic league success as well as helping to secure the European Cup. Milan was followed by Sampdoria and it wasn't long before Gullit's impressive skills and distinctive dreadlocked hair brought him to the attention of England's most successful clubs.

Gullit signed for Chelsea in 1995 and after a difficult start and a move into midfield, he finished the season as runner up to Eric Cantona for Footballer of the Year. Gullit extended his influence at Chelsea when he was appointed player-manager in 1996 and steered the club towards FA Cup success in 1997 making him the first overseas black manager to win the Cup. Gullit progressed in his managerial career but encountered difficulties and personality clashes when managing Newcastle United from 1998. He continued to manage several teams in the Netherlands and enjoyed a spell in the MLS managing LA Galaxy but found it difficult to settle.

As well as being an incredibly successful player and manager, Gullit has always been a fervent anti-apartheid supporter and friend of Nelson Mandela. He used his media presence through talk shows and interviews to raise awareness of his political views; something which he had never hidden. Gullit dedicated his Ballon d'Or award in 1987 to Nelson Mandela.

**Ruud Gullit**

**Clubs:**
HFC Haarlem, Feyenoord, PSV Eindhoven, AC Milan, Sampdoria, Chelsea.

**Holland Caps:** 100

# Chris Hughton

Chris Hughton made his debut for Tottenham Hotspur in 1979. He went on to make 398 appearances for the club in all competitions and was widely regarded as one of the best full backs of his generation. He was part of the club's two FA cup wins in 1981 and 1982 and also their 1984 UEFA cup win against Anderlecht. In his playing career Hughton also signed for West Ham and Brentford before he retired at the age of 34.

His international career was equally as impressive as he became the first mixed-race player to represent the Republic of Ireland. He won 52 caps for Ireland scoring one goal in a 6-0 win over Cyprus in a 1983 World Cup Qualifier.

In recent years Hughton has worked in numerous managerial positions. His first role came in 2009 when he led Newcastle United back into the Premier League in an impressive season; his team were unbeaten at home for the entire campaign and topped the Championship with over 100 points. In 2011 he became manager of Birmingham City, leading the team to a fourth place Championship finish, narrowly missing out on promotion. But Hughton's appointment as manager of Norwich City in June 2012, perhaps, has been his biggest role to date. In his first season of managing the Canaries, Hughton led them to an impressive 11th place finish in the Premier League; their good season typified by a 3-2 away win at Manchester City on the last day of the season. In his managerial career Chris Hughton has been one of only a few black managers working in England's top four divisions.

**Chris Hughton**

**Clubs:**
Tottenham Hotspur, West Ham Utd, Brentford.

**Rep of Ireland Caps:** 53

# Justin Fashanu

Striker Justin Fashanu - a former Dr Barnardo's boy and ABA heavyweight boxing champion - was associated with 24 different clubs (at various levels) over a period of 20 years: 1978 to 1998.

He made 444 appearances and scored 151 goals, having by far his best spells with Norwich City, for whom he made his League debut against West Bromwich Albion in January 1979, and Notts County. He scored 40 goals in 103 outings for the Canaries (winning the BBC 'Goal of the Season' award in 1980 for his stunning strike against Liverpool) and 23 in 74 games for the Magpies. He also won 11 England U21 caps.

When with Leyton Orient in 1990, Fashanu 'came out' to the press as being the first and one of only two English professional footballers to be openly gay.

The first black player to officially command a £1 million transfer fee, with his transfer from Norwich City to Nottingham Forest in 1981, Fashanu unfortunately had little success as a player after leaving The City Ground, although he continued to play and score his fair share of goals until his retirement in 1998.

Soon after moving to the United States early in 1998, he was questioned by police when a seventeen-year-old boy accused him of sexual assault, for which he was charged, and an arrest warrant was issued in Howard County, Maryland on 3rd April 1998, but he had already left his flat and fled to England where sadly he killed himself in a garage in Shoreditch, London in May 1998.

His suicide note stated he left the USA fearing he would not get a fair trial because of his homosexuality.

His brother John played for Cambridge United, Norwich, Crystal Palace, Lincoln, Millwall, Wimbledon and Aston Villa between 1977 and 1996, and gained two full England caps.

*'The first black player to be transferred for £1 million'*

**Justin Fashanu**

**Clubs:**
Norwich City, Adelaide (AUS), Notts Forest, Southampton, Notts County, Brighton, Edmonton (CAN), Man City, West Ham Utd, Leyton Orient, Torquay Utd.

# Dave Bennett

Sometimes football can be a cruel game and with the glory comes the pain, the career of Dave Bennett perfectly illustrates this point. The young Mancunian scaled the heights with Coventry City but his soccer story ended in tragedy.

David Anthony Bennett entered the world in Manchester on 11th July 1959. A talented schoolboy footballer he joined Manchester City as an apprentice on the 28th August 1976. Bennett turned pro in June 1977 but he had to wait until 14th April 1979 before he made his league debut as a substitute in a 0-0 draw against Everton at Maine Road. Under John Bond the young striker became a first team regular in the 1980/81 season which saw City and Bennett reach the FA Cup Final. The Blues played Spurs, losing 3-2 in a replay after a 1-1 draw.

Surprisingly Bennett was sold to Cardiff City in September 1981 for £120.000, joining his brother Garry who had also begun his career with Manchester City. In his first season Cardiff were Welsh Cup finalists but were relegated. The following season they were promoted. In August 1983 he moved on again when Bobby Gould signed him for First Division Coventry City for a fee of £120.000.

Bennett was a regular for the Sky Blues for the next four seasons. His moment of glory eventually came in 1987 as Coventry reached the FA Cup Final for the first time in their history. Dave had already scored a vital goal in the Semi Final victory over Leeds at Sheffield and in the Final itself he exacted revenge for 1981, scoring again as the Sky Blues triumphed over Tottenham 3-2. He seemed destined for a long career at Highfield Road, however fate took a hand and in March 1988 Dave broke his leg and he lost his first team place. A year later he joined Sheffield Wednesday who paid £250.000 for his signature.

He never recovered his form at Hillsborough and after just 31 games (8 goals) he switched to Swindon Town in September 1990. Bad luck followed him and in his second game at the County Ground he broke his leg again. Following his recovery he was loaned out to Shrewsbury Town in November 1991 and unbelievably in his second match for the Shrews at Stockport he scored twice but broke the same leg once more. He returned to Swindon and in pre season training in 1992 he broke the same leg for the third time, an accident that finished a career which had held such promise when he lifted the Cup for Coventry in 1987. Football can indeed be a cruel game.

### Dave Bennett

**Clubs:**
Man City, Cardiff City, Coventry City
Sheffield Wednesday, Swindon Town,
Shrewsbury Town.

# Subbuteo

In 1946 in Tunbridge Wells, young Peter Adolph with the help of wire, paper nets, cardboard figures, chalk and an old army jacket developed the basis of the table soccer game that was to become Subbuteo.

The period after the Second World War was boom time for football as fans of the game attended in droves to see goal laden matches. Peter Adolph's game reflected the popularity of the sport so much so that over the next two decades Subbuteo table soccer became a national obsession and an international success story.

In 1966 the World Cup Finals took place in England and Subbuteo issued sets of the sixteen competing teams featuring hand painted miniature figures in their respective strips. From this point on international teams became a part of the Subbuteo brand.

By 1980 Subbuteo had taken hold in over fifty countries world wide where over ten million enthusiasts played the game. From its humble beginnings of cardboard figures and chalk pitches it had grown to the point where you could buy spectators, green cloth pitches, terracing, floodlights and a myriad of other accessories. The table top version of Soccer reflected the trends and the development of the real game. At the end of 1980 there were 750 teams available in the Subbuteo catalogue.

In the late 70's in England the domestic game began to see the rise of black players to a position of prominence. In 1978 West Bromwich Albion were blazing a trail to the top of the First Division with a team that displayed attacking flair and a brand of exciting football which captured the football world's imagination. Unusually for the domestic game at that time that side included three black players. Full back Brendon Batson, winger Laurie Cunningham and centre forward Cyrille Regis. Albion's bright young manager Ron Atkinson, christened the black players the 'Three Degrees' after a popular female singing trio who were high in the pop charts. Whilst the young ladies harmonised off the field Albion's three young black players harmonised on it.

Prior to 1978 Subbuteo had issued international team sets such as Brazil, Argentina, Portugal, Chile and Uruguay which featured black figures and in 1978 the iconic game gave the Three Degrees the ultimate accolade when they issued a West Bromwich Albion team set which became the first English Subbuteo miniature set to include three black figures. Batson wearing number two, Regis number nine and Cunningham number 11.

Arguably this bold move by Subbuteo gave notice to the football world and the millions of 'flick to kick' fans that black players had finally arrived in the English game paving the way for hundreds of black footballers to follow.

# Laurie Cunningham

Laurie Cunningham was one of the most influential and gifted black British footballers ever to grace English football.

A silky skilled winger, Cunningham was a true pioneer - the first of West Brom's so-called Three Degrees to join the Black County club in 1977, the first black player to represent England at under 21 level and the first black player to leave England for a career on the continent at Spanish giants, Real Madrid, in 1979.

Best remembered for his two year spell at The Hawthorns, Cunningham electrified crowds with his pace, grace and control - scoring 21 goals in 86 appearances for West Brom but more memorably partnering Cyrille Regis and Brendon Batson as the first trio of black players at a top flight, successful club.

This radical step changed English football - initially drawing racist taunts from opposing crowds, but also winning hearts and minds with class and courage, and ultimately providing inspiration for subsequent generations of black players who emulated Regis and Cunningham on school playgrounds across Britain.

Cunningham's career began at Leyton Orient in 1974 where he bagged 15 goals in 75 appearances before moving to First Division West Brom for £130,000 in March 1977.

His first full season with Albion in 1977-78 saw them finish sixth in the First Division to earn a place in the following season's UEFA Cup.

In a team of rising stars including Regis, Bryan Robson, Derek Statham and club record goal scorer Tony Brown, Albion cruised to the top of the First Division in 1978/79, inspired by several outstanding Cunningham performances most notably in wins at Chelsea, Leeds, Arsenal, Wolves and in particular a 5-3 televised thumping of Manchester United.

Laurie's scintillating performance at Valencia in a UEFA CUP tie (shown live on Spanish TV) attracted the attention of Real Madrid, who signed him the following summer for £950,000.

## 'The first black player to represent England in a full international'

Cunningham had made his full England debut (the first of six England caps) at the culmination of an ultimately frustrating season as Albion's title challenge wilted amid the winter snow, which led to a dreadful fixture backlog and saw them ultimately finish third.

Cunningham shone briefly at Real Madrid but his five-year stint at the Bernabeu was marred by injury. He made just 44 appearances, scoring 13 goals, before embarking on a nomadic journey including loan spells at Manchester United and Sporting Gijon, and moves to Marseille, Leicester City, Rayo Vallecano, Charleroi and, bizarrely, Wimbledon - at the time known as English football's Crazy Gang - where he won an FA Cup Winners medal in 1988.

Cunningham died in a car crash in Madrid in July 1989 at the age of just 33.

His cherished memory lives on as a pioneer of the game to be immortalised with the Celebration 1979 statue featuring Cyrille Regis and Brendon Batson to be unveiled in West Bromwich in 2015.

### Laurie Cunningham

**Clubs:**
Leyton Orient, West Bromwich Albion, Real Madrid (ESP), Sporting Gijon, Rayo Vallecano, Man Utd, Marseille, Leicester, RSC Charleroi (BEL), Wimbledon.

**England Caps:** 6

# Cyrille Regis

Cyrille Regis is a true football legend.

An exciting, prolific and whole-hearted centre-forward, Regis was a scorer of spectacular goals and an inspiration for generations of black British players, notably during his seven year career with West Bromwich Albion between 1977-1984.

Born in French Guiana, but growing up in London, Regis had seemingly missed the boat on a professional football career until he was spotted playing Sunday football in Regents Park as a 17-year-old by John Sullivan, chairman of Surrey-based non-League club, Molesey.

After single seasons at Molesey and fellow non-Leaguers Hayes, Regis was snapped up by First Division West Bromwich Albion for just £5,000 in May 1977.

Albion scout and soon-to-be manager Ronnie Allen, a former England and Albion centre-forward, was so convinced of the young player's talent that he offered to buy him with his own money.

A Roy of the Rovers style debut in a League Cup tie against Rotherham in September 1977 in which Regis scored twice and left the pitch with the crowd chanting his name was followed by a wonder goal on his league debut against Middlesbrough three days later.

Significantly Regis struck up a near telepathic relationship with fellow black forward Laurie Cunningham. When they were joined by a third black player, defender Brendon Batson, they were given the uncomfortable moniker of the Three Degrees. Three black players at one club was unheard of at the time and the trio were targeted for racist abuse during games.

Regis won PFA Young Player of the Year in 1978 and went on to play for the England Under-21 and senior national teams. In total, he scored 112 goals in 297 appearances for West Brom before joining Coventry City for £250,000 in 1984.

Although he was less prolific for the Sky Blues (62 goals in 274 appearances), Regis won the only trophy of his career at Coventry – an FA Cup winners medal in 1987.

A smattering of goals for Aston Villa, Wolves, Wycombe Wanderers and Chester City rounded off a distinguished 19 year professional career which ended in 1996.

Regis returned to The Hawthorns as a coach before becoming a football agent.

In 2008 Regis was awarded an MBE. He also has an honourary doctorate from the University of Wolverhampton and is an ambassador for the charity Water Aid. His autobiography, Cyrille Regis - My Story, was published to widespread acclaim in 2010.

In 2015, a permanent memorial to the Three Degrees will be unveiled in West Bromwich town centre.

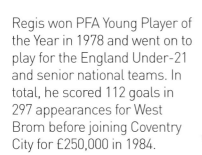

## Cyrille Regis

**Clubs:**
West Bromwich Albion, Coventry City,
Aston Villa, Wolves,
Wycombe Wanderers, Chester City.

**England Caps:** 5

# Brendon Batson

Brendon Batson was a respected top flight professional footballer, most notably with West Bromwich Albion where, as an accomplished full back, he was known as one of the club's so-called Three Degrees.

As an administrator, he has arguably achieved more than any other black British former player.

Originally from Grenada, Batson's family moved to London in 1962 when he was nine-years-old. Batson hadn't seen or played football before - but by 16 was good enough to be taken on as an apprentice by Arsenal in 1971.

A natural leader with a robust physique, he became Arsenal's first ever black player, making his first team debut for the Gunners at the age of 18 (ironically against the club he would later join and be most closely associated with, West Bromwich Albion).

After ten appearances in three seasons at Highbury, Brendon moved to Cambridge United in 1974 where he spent four years and became first team captain under U's manager Ron Atkinson.

When Atkinson took the reins at West Brom in January 1978, Batson followed as his first signing for £30,000 - a miniscule fee for a cultured right back who would soon make three England B team appearances and knock on the door of the England senior team.

*'Arsenal's first black player'*

At West Brom, Batson joined fellow black British players Laurie Cunningham and Cyrille Regis, a radical step at the time as no top flight club had previously fielded three black players in one team.

The reaction from fans was mixed. They were admired as skilful, brave and inspirational players who ignored racist taunts by opposing fans to play some of the most attractive football of their generation.

Sadly, the Three Degrees candle shone all too briefly. Cunningham moved to Real Madrid in 1979 and Batson's career was ended by a knee injury in 1982 at the age of 29 - ironically at a time when he was in the best form of his career.

In total he made 345 first team appearances including 172 for the Baggies - but Batson's football career was far from finished as a career in administration and management beckoned.

Batson worked for the Professional Footballers' Association (PFA) eventually becoming deputy chief executive.

In 2000 he was awarded an MBE for services to football but left the PFA in 2002 to re-join West Brom as managing director - a role which saw Batson become the first black senior executive at an English football club. He left two years later to pursue a career as a football consultant.

The impact and influence of the Three Degrees will be immortalised in a statue to be unveiled in West Bromwich town centre in spring 2015.

**Brendon Batson**

Clubs:
Arsenal, Cambridge Utd,
West Bromwich Albion.

# An All-Black Team

**LEN CANTELLO**

LEN CANTELLO TESTIMONIAL MATCH.    DONATION 15p.
WEST BROMWICH ALBION XI v CYRILLE REGIS & LAURIE CUNNINGHAM XI
At THE HAWTHORNS — Tuesday 15th May, 1979 — Kick-off 7.30 p.m.

The Len Cantello testimonial committee in 1979 had many meetings and the talk of a match was high on the agenda. But who would be the chosen opponents? Teams such as Aston Villa, Wolves and even Manchester United were mentioned but in the end - with some input from Albion's 'Three Degrees', Brendon Batson, Cyrille Regis and Laurie Cunningham, it was decided unanimously to get together an all-Black XI to play Albion at The Hawthorns.

At the time, there were well over 30 black footballers registered with Football League clubs up and down the country and following another meeting, it was agreed that Cyrille would captain a selected All Black XI against Len's Albion team. It was as simple as that!

Phone calls were made, personal meetings set up, and in less than three months, early in 1979, a squad of 20 black players had been drawn up from all over the country. The organisers concentrated initially on those players who were situated within a 60-mile radius of West Bromwich - to save travelling. And if fit and available, no-one declined to play... some further afield offered their services as well.

There was a lot of paper talk surrounding the game, but nothing was at all detrimental and to have an All-Black football team playing together was something new.

## 'It was a triumph which, if anything, struck a blow for multiculturalism'

The late 1970's was a pre Kick It Out era that appeared to have no answer to the scourge of racism, with black players routinely suffering abuse that went shamefully unchecked.

It was in such a climate that Cantello's willing helpers decided there should be just one stipulation about those lining up against him for his testimonial game. They had to be black.

Cyrille Regis, Laurie Cunningham, and Brendon Batson were charged with bringing the idea to fruition, and the 'All Blacks', as they were referred to in the local paper's match report the following day, duly stepped out to face an all-white Cantello XI at the Hawthorns on May 15th 1979.

It finished 3-2 to Cyrille's team but the result that mattered most was how the concept was embraced by players of both sides and the people of Sandwell, 7,023 of whom paid to see it.

According to Batson, it was a triumph which, if anything, struck a blow for multiculturalism.

"One or two people afterwards said it could have been divisive, but that was the only time anyone ever questioned it or expressed any misgivings," recalled Batson.

Back row, left to right: Ian Benjamin (Sheffield Utd), Vernon Hodgson (WBA), Brendon Batson (WBA), Derek Richardson (QPR), Stewart Phillips (Hereford Utd), George Berry (Wolves), Garth Crooks (Stoke City).
Front row,: Winston White (Hereford Utd), Cyrille Regis (WBA), Laurie Cunningham (WBA), Remi Moses (WBA), Valmore Thomas (Hereford Utd)

# Bobby Barnes

Bobby Barnes was a quick, skillful winger who began his career as an apprentice with West Ham United, the team that he supported as a boy.

He won a FA Youth Cup winners medal in 1981 and was capped for England at youth level before turning professional with West Ham in September 1980. Bobby scored on his League debut against Watford in September 1980 and went on to make 43 league appearances in six seasons, scoring five goals. He joined Aldershot in March 1986 for a fee of £15,000 and was an immediate success with his new club scoring 26 goals in 49 league games and helping Aldershot to promotion through the first ever Third Division play-offs in 1987.

In October 1987, Barnes moved to Second Division side Swindon Town for a fee of £50,000 in a deal that also saw Steve Berry go in the other direction. He scored in six successive league games between October and December 1988, and went on to make over 40 league appearances, scoring 13 times for Swindon.

Bobby joined Bournemouth for a fee of £110,000 in March 1989 but after only 14 games he was sold to Northampton Town for £70,000.

Barnes managed to star despite Northampton being relegated, and with Tony Adcock formed a successful striking partnership with Bobby scoring 37 times in 98 league games for the Cobblers.

In February 1992 Bobby moved to Peterborough were he played 49 times scoring nine goals and winning promotion to the First Division beating Stockport in a Wembley play-off in 1992.

After retiring in 1996, Barnes joined the Professional Footballers Association full-time and he is now Deputy Chief Executive. Bobby is also a staunch supporter of the Show Racism the Red Card campaign and was inducted into their Hall of Fame in 2008.

**KICK IT OUT**
TACKLING RACISM & DISCRIMINATION

## Bobby Barnes

**Clubs:**
West Ham Utd, Scunthorpe Utd, Aldershot Town, Swindon Town, Bournemouth, Northampton Town, Peterborough Utd, Torquay Utd, Partick Thistle.

# Danny Wallace

Danny Wallace was born on 21st January 1964 and he was one of the country's brightest young sports stars when he signed for Southampton in 1982 aged just 16. Wallace was a spirited player and full of energy. His 5'4" frame didn't stop him from cutting swathes through Division One defences. Wallace went on to claim the Goal of the Season award in 1983/4.

During his time at Southampton, Wallace was selected for his only England International appearance and scored in the 1-1 draw against Egypt.

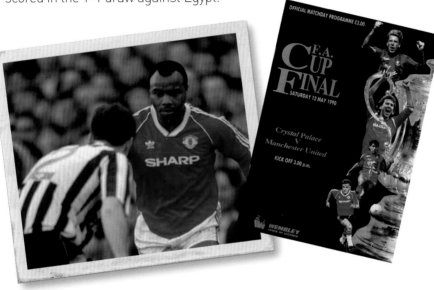

Wallace played alongside his brothers Ray and Rod for Southampton – the only time three brothers had been fielded together in top flight football since 1920. Wallace signed for Manchester United in 1989 and went on to help the club to FA Cup glory in 1990 and the European Cup Winners Cup the following season.

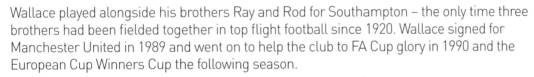

Wallace's flying start at United was hampered by a number of small injuries which he seemed to be suffering more frequently. In 1993, Wallace was transferred to Birmingham City on an 18-month deal, but he managed only 12 games during that time because of regular injury. It wasn't until 1996 that Wallace discovered that his unfortunate spate of injuries was due to him suffering from multiple sclerosis.

Following diagnosis, Wallace suffered from deep depression, which took him almost five years to begin to recover from. Since then, he has been able to turn his efforts and fighting spirit towards other causes. He is now an active fundraiser for the MS Society. His testimonial in 2004 saw the likes of Viv Anderson, Matthew Le Tissier and Paul Ince turn out to play and raise funds to support the MS Society.

Wallace enriched people's lives as a player and continues to do so as a role model for MS sufferers and young black footballers.

## Danny Wallace

**Clubs:**
Southampton, Manchester Utd, Millwall, Birmingham City, Wycombe Wanderers.

**England Caps:** 1

# John Barnes

If there was a vote to decide on England's finest goal, there is a fair chance that John Barnes would win it. In June 1984, Barnes made his tenth appearance for England and scored his first goal for his country. And what a goal it was. England beat Brazil 2-0 in front of 56,000 fans at the Maracana Stadium in Rio and just before half time Barnes went on a forty-yard run, jinking past Brazilian defenders, before drawing the goalie and calmly shooting home to give England the lead. It was a magnificent goal, a goal even the great Pele would have been proud of. It brought Barnes to international prominence, whatever the Watford man did in the rest of his career Barnes had his place in history: a black player scoring one of England's greatest goals.

John Charles Bryan Barnes was born in Kingston, Jamaica on 7th November 1963. His father was Roderick Kenrick 'Ken' Barnes. Roderick played football, squash, and was an accomplished swimmer. From an early age, John's interest in football was fostered by Roderick who also instituted a sense of discipline into his sons life.

In 1976 the Barnes family moved to London, where John played for the Stowe Boys Club in Paddington. From there he progressed to Sudbury Court F.C. in the Middlesex League, where he was spotted by Watford. After a trial with the Hornets he signed for them on 14th July 1981.

Barnes made his Watford debut as a 17-year-old substitute in a Second Division match against Oldham Athletic in a 1-1 draw at Vicarage Road on 3rd September 1981. In his first season at Watford he scored 13 goals in 36 league games as the Hornets were promoted to Division One.

*'Barnes had his place in history, a black player scoring one of England's finest goals'*

The following season he was an ever-present (42 league games), netting ten times as Watford finished in second place behind Liverpool in Division One. John had rapidly developed into a top class player with his graceful style, pace, passing ability and a powerful shot. In May 1983 he gained his first England cap as a substitute in a 0-0 draw against Northern Ireland in Belfast.

In May 1984, Barnes played in his first FA Cup final at Wembley, as Watford lost 2-0 to Everton and although John finished on the losing side, there were many more better days to come.

Barnes' career at Watford blossomed and as a result on 19th June 1987, he moved to Liverpool for a fee of £900,000.

In his debut season at Anfield, Barnes' Liverpool won the League Championship and were runners up in the FA Cup where they were beaten at Wembley by underdogs Wimbledon, thus he picked up his second losers medal. By way of consolation, John was such a success at Anfield that he was voted Footballer of the Year and also the PFA Player of the Year.

1989 will always be remembered by Liverpool fans for two pivotal moments in their long and proud history. Although they won the FA Cup at Wembley, defeating Everton 3-2, they had to suffer the huge disappointment of losing the League title on the last night of the season to Arsenal at Anfield. That upset paled into insignificance compared to the events of Hillsborough in the Semi-Final of the Cup on April 15th 1989, when 96 Liverpool fans lost their lives in the opening minutes of the game against Nottingham Forest. In the aftermath that followed, Barnes, along with his Liverpool team mates, was a mourner at a number of the funerals of the victims of the Hillsborough disaster.

In 1989-90, John gained his second League Championship medal as Liverpool won the title. Barnes was an England regular under Bobby Robson but his role at Liverpool and with the national side changed. The arrival of Graeme Souness as manager at Anfield was the catalyst for this change. Although he made John club captain, he switched him from his left wing position into midfield and gradually John became less effective and suffered a number of injuries, which affected his form.

On 25th May 1991, Barnes won the last of his 79 England caps (ten goals) against Argentina in a 2-2 draw at Wembley. John was 27 years old. The goal he had scored at the Maracana had been the pinnacle of his England adventure, setting a standard which was almost impossible to maintain.

His swansong at Anfield came in 1995 when he won a League Cup Winners medal for Liverpool who defeated Bolton Wanderers 2-1 at Wembley. In August 1997 he joined Newcastle United on a free transfer. He had an indifferent time at St James' Park playing just 26 league matches for them (six goals). He moved to Charlton Athletic in 1998 and after just 12 league appearances for the Addicks he retired in the Summer of 1999. John had a brief but unsuccessful flirtation with management at Celtic and Tranmere Rovers and also coached the Jamaican National side.

It is fair to say that during his career Barnes saw both triumph and tragedy. In his early days at Liverpool he faced racial abuse from opposition fans and opponents on the field. John faced it with dignity and self discipline. Following a career of ups and downs, Barnes leaves a legacy which includes that wonderful goal against Brazil, two footballer of the year awards, an MBE in 1998 and almost the ultimate accolade when, in 2005, he received 110,000 votes in an Anfield poll which saw him placed fifth in the top 100 Liverpool players of all time. A fitting tribute to a man who helped to establish the continuing success of black players on Merseyside and the English national side.

**John Barnes**

**Clubs:**
Watford, Liverpool, Newcastle Utd, Charlton Athletic.
**England Caps:** 79

# Paul McGrath

Paul McGrath's story is a true rags to riches tale. He was born in Ealing on 4th December 1959, but when he was two months old his mother took him to Monkstown in County Dublin. His football career began with junior side Pearse Rovers before he switched to Leinster Senior League side Dalkey United. In the autumn of 1981 Paul made the step up to the League of Ireland side St. Patricks Athletic. Here he was nicknamed 'The Black Pearl of Inchicore' and in 1981/82 he was voted PFAI Player of the Year.

In April 1982 Ron Atkinson paid out £30,000 plus add ons to take the giant Irishman to Manchester United. He made his league debut in November 1982 against Spurs at Old Trafford. Paul gained a regular spot for United in the second half of the 1984/85 season which also coincided with his first cap for the Republic of Ireland on 5th of February 1985 when he appeared as a substitute against Italy in a 2-1 defeat in Dublin.

At over six feet tall he was at home in either defence or midfield where his pace and poise became the mainstays of his game. In May 1985 he gave a classy performance as ten man United beat favourites Everton in the FA Cup final. In 1987 he was the man of the match for the Football league in a showpiece friendly against the Rest of the World to celebrate the League's Centenary. His display against Diego Maradona brought him to the attention of Europe's top teams.

His career at United took a downturn when a series of knee injuries and some well publicised off field problems halted his progress and following a disagreement with the management he put in a transfer request. Any potential move was scuppered by a series of cartilage operations and although he broke back into the Red Devils' first team, now managed by Alex Ferguson, another serious misdemeanour saw 'Fergie' run out of patience with Paul, and in the summer of 1989 Graham Taylor took him to Aston Villa for £450,000.

His career with Ireland had fared a little better, under Jack Charlton Paul played in the 1988 European Championship Finals but it was at Villa that McGrath blossomed. His dodgy knees hampered his training but on match days at Villa Park he played like a superman. In his initial season at the Villa they finished runners up to Liverpool and he went on to win Villa's player of the year award four seasons on the trot. In 1992/93 Villa finished runners up again and Paul was voted PFA player of the season.

In 1994 and 1996 he helped Villa to win the League Cup against his former club Manchester United and Leeds respectively. In the same period Paul starred for the Republic of Ireland in the World Cup Finals of 1990 and 1994. His display against Italy in New York in 1994 is viewed as one of the greatest by any Irishman in the green shirt. The Irish won 1-0 and Paul McGrath subdued the great Roberto Baggio to give the Republic one of the major triumphs in their history.

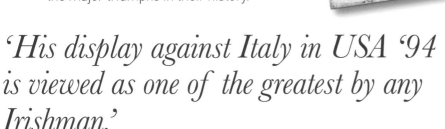

## 'His display against Italy in USA '94 is viewed as one of the greatest by any Irishman.'

Having played the best football of his career in Claret and Blue he left Villa Park for Derby in 1996 and in February 1997 he won the last of his 83 caps in a 0-0 draw at Cardiff against Wales, bringing down the curtain on a fabulous international career.

Following his brief spell at Derby he signed for Sheffield United where he played his last League game at Ipswich on 9th November 1997.

Paul McGrath is in the top fifty greatest Irish players of all time and is also regarded as one of Villa's finest players. From his humble beginnings "The Black Pearl of Inchicore" went on to play in the Premier League and to star in the World Cup, the greatest stage in the world for one of the finest black players these islands have ever produced.

**Paul McGrath**

**Clubs:**
St. Patricks, Man Utd, Aston Villa, Derby County, Sheffield Utd.

**Republic of Ireland Caps:** 83

# Paul Ince

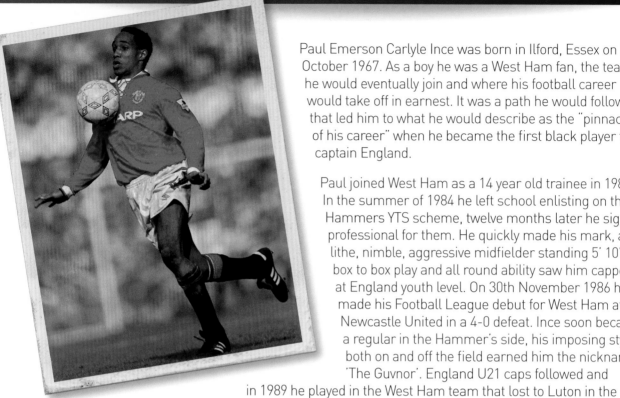

Paul Emerson Carlyle Ince was born in Ilford, Essex on 21st October 1967. As a boy he was a West Ham fan, the team he would eventually join and where his football career would take off in earnest. It was a path he would follow that led him to what he would describe as the "pinnacle of his career" when he became the first black player to captain England.

Paul joined West Ham as a 14 year old trainee in 1981. In the summer of 1984 he left school enlisting on the Hammers YTS scheme, twelve months later he signed professional for them. He quickly made his mark, a lithe, nimble, aggressive midfielder standing 5' 10" his box to box play and all round ability saw him capped at England youth level. On 30th November 1986 he made his Football League debut for West Ham at Newcastle United in a 4-0 defeat. Ince soon became a regular in the Hammer's side, his imposing style both on and off the field earned him the nickname 'The Guvnor'. England U21 caps followed and in 1989 he played in the West Ham team that lost to Luton in the League Cup Semi Final and at the end of that season West Ham were relegated.

In the summer of 1989 to the displeasure and angst of the West Ham fans Paul signed for Manchester United for £1.7 million in a protracted deal which was held up because of a pelvic problem that saw the initial transfer fee reduced. He was an instant success at Old Trafford winning a Cup winner's medal in his first season as the Reds drew 3-3 with Crystal Palace, then won the replay 1-0, a game in which Ince played right back and won a man of the match award.

In 1991 Paul starred alongside Bryan Robson as United won the European Cup Winners Cup beating Barcelona. The Red Devils won the League Cup in 1992. On 7th September 1992 he won his first England Cap in Santander in a 1-0 reversal against Spain and by the end of the 1992-93 season, his star was truly in the ascendancy as United won the Premier League for the first time. To complete his meteoric rise to fame Paul became the first black player to captain England in a 2-0 defeat to the USA in Boston on 9th June 1993. In all he won 53 caps for his country, skippering them seven times.

The trophies continued to pile up at Old Trafford. By now Paul had taken over the mantle of midfield general from the legendary Bryan Robson. In 1993-94 Ince and United swept all before winning the League and Cup double. Early in his career Paul had been a fiery character sometimes marred by controversy but this achievement saw him mature as a player and a person to become one of the dominant characters in English football.

In 1995 United lost in the FA Cup final to Everton and also missed out on the Premier League Title. United fans viewed the season as a disaster but their disappointment was compounded when, following rumours that Ince and Ferguson had fallen out the United Manager, enforcing his authority once more, sold his star midfielder to Inter Milan for £7.5 million in the summer of 1995.

Paul's stay in Milan was brief. In May 1996 he was in the Inter side that lost 4-1 on penalties to Schalke 04 in the UEFA Cup Final. Whilst at the San Siro he was part of the England team that reached the Semi Finals of the European Championships in 1996. At the end of the 1996-97 season he turned down the chance of staying in Italy and decided to join Liverpool for a fee of £4.2 million. The Liverpool manager Roy Evans declared that he had a new leader and made Ince his club captain at Anfield.

Apart from a brief spell when he teamed up with Jamie Redknapp in a solid midfield partnership his time at Anfield was disrupted by injury and spats on and off the pitch. New Liverpool boss Gérard Houllier quickly dealt with the matter when he took over and sold Paul to Middlesbrough in August 1999 for £1 million.

Ince had turned out for England in the 1998 World Cup Finals, at the Riverside he was reunited with his old England skipper Bryan Robson and for three seasons he was instrumental in keeping the "Boro" in the Premier league. Job done, in 2002 he moved to Wolves and promptly helped them into the Premier League leading them to victory in the Play Off Final at Cardiff where they beat Sheffield United 3-0. With the Wanderers he managed another 35 League games in the top flight and passed the milestone of 700 games in his club career.

## 'The first black player to captain England'

He left Molineux in 2006 and very briefly played for Swindon and Macclesfield (where he made his last ever appearance as a pro in a 1-1 draw at home to Notts County on 5th May 2007). Thereafter in 2007-8 he piloted Milton Keynes Dons to a 2-0 victory over Grimsby in the Final of the Football League Trophy and to the League Two Championship. This success was rewarded when on 22nd August 2008 he was appointed Manager of Premier League side Blackburn Rovers. Paul Ince thus created another piece of history becoming the first black Manager ever in the top flight of English football. Sadly it was not a success and after just three wins in 17 games he was sacked from his post on 16th December 2008. Since then he has had spells at MK Dons, Notts County and Blackpool where he lost his job on 21st January 2014.

Paul Ince had a marvellous playing career which resulted in the ultimate accolade of being the first black player to captain England, a feat which will remain unsurpassed for perpetuity. His son Thomas is a fine prospect having already played for the England Under 21 side and it may not be too long before an Ince plays for the full England side again.

### Paul Ince

**Clubs:**
West Ham Utd, Manchester Utd, Inter Milan, Liverpool, Middlesbrough, Wolves, Swindon, Macclesfield Town.

**England Caps:** 53

# Brian Deane

Although Brian Deane was born in Leeds in 1968 and represented his home town at schoolboy and youth levels, his professional career actually commenced at Doncaster Rovers in the lower reaches of the English Football League. He made his professional debut for them in 1985 and played over sixty games across a three year period, scoring a modest number of goals in the process, before being signed by Sheffield United in 1988.

There he made significant progress as a tall and 'bustling' type of centre-forward, who as well as posing a real aerial threat to opposing teams also worried them with his intelligent play, attitude and impressive strong turn of pace. Combined with his powerful physical presence, creditable work-rate and 'good feet' capable of delicate skill on the ball, he was frequently the focal point of Sheffield United's direct style of attacking play and became a firm favourite of the fans. On Saturday 15th August, 1992, at around 3.05pm and just five minutes in to the game, Brian instinctively headed what memorably was the very first goal ever scored in the Premier League, against Manchester United.

## 'The scorer of the very first Premier League goal'

While at the Blades he was capped three times by the England 'B' team before moving up the scale to make three appearances for the full England side. He joined Leeds United for £2.9 million in June 1993 in what was a record transfer fee for both the buying club and the selling club. Other clubs he later went on to play for include Benfica, Middlesbrough, Leicester City and West Ham United but it is at Bramall Lane and then Elland Road where he really made his name as a striker of note.

In his professional playing career he played over 600 times and scored nearly 200 goals. He is currently in charge of Sarpsborg in Norway where he is steadily establishing himself as a good young manager.

### Brian Deane

**Clubs:**
Doncaster Rovers, Sheffield Utd, Leeds Utd, Benfica (POR), Middlesbrough, Leicester City, West Ham Utd.

**England Caps:** 3

# Michael Thomas

Arguably Michael Thomas scored one of the most famous goals by a black footballer in the history of the game and it would give him immortality.

Michael Lauriston Thomas was born in Lambeth, London on 24th August 1967. He joined Arsenal as a schoolboy in 1982 and turned professional for the Gunners on 31st December 1984. In January 1987 he was loaned out to Portsmouth where he played three games and on 8th February 1987 he made his Arsenal debut in a first leg League Cup semi final match at Highbury against Spurs. The Gunners lost 1-0 but won the second leg. He followed this with his league debut against Sheffield Wednesday on 14th February. He won a League Cup winners medal on 5th April 1987 as a sub in the Final against Liverpool.

1989 was to be his year of destiny. Thomas was now a regular in midfield for Arsenal and on the last evening of the 1988/89 season on 26th May, Arsenal travelled to Anfield for a title decider against Liverpool (a match which had been rearranged due to the Hillsborogh disaster). Just a draw would have been enough for the Reds and they could even afford to lose by one goal and still be Champions. If Arsenal won by a two goal margin they would be title winners. With one minute to go Arsenal were a goal up, Alan Smith flicked a ball on to Thomas who shot past Grobbelaar to give the Gunners a 2-0 win and take the Title to Highbury.

Michael spent two more years at Arsenal winning a second league title in 1991 and two full England caps which meant he had been honoured at five different levels for England, the first Gunner to achieve this feat.

On 16th December 1991 after 206 games and 30 goals, Thomas joined Liverpool for a fee of £1.5 million and in his first season at Anfield he won an FA Cup winners medal scoring a 'classic' cup final goal in the Reds 2-0 win over Sunderland in 1992. He was never a regular at Anfield but he was a League Cup Winner again in 1995 when Liverpool defeated Bolton at Wembley. In 1998 he had a short loan spell at Middlesbrough before moving on 1st August 1998 to Benfica where he had a brief fruitless sojourn until July 2000 when he signed for Wimbledon. Twelve months later in May 2001 he retired from the game.

Michael Thomas now runs a security firm in Liverpool (Stop Taking The Michael) but he will always be remembered for the goal that robbed Liverpool of the League Championship and took it to Highbury. A truly historical strike which inspired a book and a film – "Fever Pitch" by Gooner Nick Hornby. Top that!

MICHAEL THOMAS

## Michael Thomas

**Clubs:**
Arsenal, Portsmouth, Liverpool. Middlesbrough, Wimbledon, Benfica (POR).
**England Caps:** 2

# Les Ferdinand

Les Ferdinand was born on 8th December 1966 in England. He started his football career at non-league Hayes, before being signed by Queens Park Rangers in 1987, where he built an impressive record, scoring 80 goals in 163 appearances.

Ferdinand is recognised for his contributions both in league play and internationally being the only player to score for 6 different Premier League clubs.

Only the signing of a big striker could satisfy the disillusioned Tottenham faithful after Teddy Sheringham moved to Manchester United in July 1997. When Ferdinand arrived from Newcastle the following month, that's exactly what they got. A player with a proven scoring record, Ferdinand was blessed with the lightening pace that Sheringham lacked, as well as an astonishing leap for a man under six feet.

Although the £6m price tag was undoubtedly high for a 30-year-old, the money looked to be well spent when the solidly built striker scored three times in the first four games, including a brace to help defeat Aston Villa 3-2. Yet Ferdinand missed much of the 1997-98 campaign through injury. Ferdinand's contribution later in the season helped save Spurs from relegation in 1997/98 and to win the League Cup in 1999.

Ferdinand was capped 17 times for England and went on to enjoy a successful career as a football coach at Tottenham after retiring from playing.

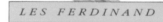

LES FERDINAND

## Les Ferdinand

**Clubs:**
Queens Park Rangers, Brentford, Newcastle Utd, Tottenham Hotspur, West Ham Utd, Leicester City, Bolton Wanderers, Reading.

**England Caps:** 17

# Kevin Campbell

Kevin Campbell was a strong footballer from an early age and joined the Arsenal youth team in 1985 at the age of 15. Campbell had a great run on the youth team and scored 59 goals in a season, helping the team to FA Youth Cup victory.

It was 1988 when Campbell made his debut for the Arsenal first team, but he was not able to secure himself a permanent spot as a forward in the team. Campbell made a great impression on Frank Clark, manager of Leyton Orient while on loan to the club in 1989 where he scored nine goals in 16 games. Campbell had a further loan spell at Leicester City before establishing himself fully in the Arsenal team in 1990/91 scoring an amazing eight times in ten games.

Campbell was always a strong forward, but his position was challenged within the team by other incredibly talented attacking players. Campbell's best season for the Gunners was 1992/93 when he managed 19 goals in a season. Campbell played a total of 224 games scoring 59 goals for Arsenal before his form started to wane in 1994/95.

Seasons at Nottingham Forest and Turkish side Trabzonspor followed for Campbell. He was only at the Turkish club for a very short time, though he established himself as a favourite with team mates and fans alike. The season was turned sour for Campbell when he was racially abused by the president of Trabzonspor who called him a "discoloured cannibal". Campbell was supported by his Turkish team mates when he described this incident in the press conference that saw him leave the team.

Campbell made a great recovery from this incredibly disappointing experience when he joined Everton on loan in 1999. He scored nine goals in eight games making him Everton's top goal scorer that season and winning him the player of the season award – the first on-loan player ever to win it. This was followed by two more seasons as Everton's top goal scorer before a free transfer to West Bromwich Albion in 2005. Campbell became team captain shortly after arriving at the Hawthorns and went on to help WBA survive relegation from the Premiership.

Campbell also had a fruitful international career as well, earning 4 caps for the England U21 team and one for England's B team. He stands out as the English player who has scored the most goals in the Premier League without earning an England cap.

Campbell is an inspiration to young black players as he conducted himself with strength, dedication and courage in the face of racism from within his own team. He flourished in his goal scoring career and earned an enviable reputation as a passionate and reliable forward.

## Kevin Campbell

**Clubs:**
Arsenal, Leyton Orient, Leicester, Notts Forest, Trabzonspor, Everton, West Bromwich Albion, Cardiff City.

# Lucas Radebe

Lucas Radebe, born on 12th April 1969 in Soweto, South Africa, is probably the most famous South African footballer ever. He is almost certainly the only footballer to have a renowned rock band named in his honour!

1969 was of course during the shameful rule of apartheid but politics rarely stops youngsters trying to enjoy themselves... as a child, Lucas played football, lots of it, though more often than not he was in goal rather than outfield. His 'gangly' physique and razor-sharp reflexes ensured he was good at it too. Amazingly, in his early teens, he would suffer a gun shot wound. Shootings were relatively common but it was in fact a random incident, with no indication of who was actually responsible for the shooting or as to why it happened. Thankfully the wound proved not to be life-threatening and with no permanent effects, even though the bullet had initially entered his lower back. He would be back playing football within a short space of time!

Eventually he moved out of goal and, at first, in to central midfield. Youth teams he played for were Diepkloof Wolf Wanderers, ICL Birds and finally Kaizer Chiefs juniors. Versatility and willingness to learn are great qualities in football, and Lucas Radebe always possessed such qualities meaning that while learning the trade of midfielder he was also observing how to be a commander in defence at the same time. Kaizer Chiefs signed him on professional terms and 1989 saw his debut. In five years he would play 113 times for the Chiefs, scoring five goals in total.

In 1994, along with striker Philemon Masinga, Lucas was sold to Premier League club Leeds United, managed by Howard Wilkinson, for a combined fee of £250,000. It was not a particularly noteworthy deal and, in truth, their early days were hardly successful or happy ones. Although Wilkinson had given Lucas his chance in English football, it was the manager's successor George Graham who helped his career to really flourish. And Graham's own successor, David O'Leary, was equally impressed by the player's consistency and leadership, crucial attributes in a period of Leeds building a side based around youth and academy players. In 1998 Lucas was made team captain, the first black player to be given the honour and the first foreign player also. He always led – on and off the pitch - by example, demonstrating tremendous skill, leadership and a classic sporting chivalry typical of a real gentleman. He even filled in for sent-off 'keepers in two Leeds games, and showed he still possessed safe hands!

## "Lucas Radebe is my hero"

Nelson Mandela

In 2000 he was awarded the FIFA Fair Play Award, another sign of his popularity in the world of football, and was made captain of the South African national team, for whom he played a total of 70 matches. And a certain band from Leeds decided to call themselves The Kaiser Chiefs in tribute to Lucas 'The Chief' Radebe. In eleven years at Leeds, Lucas would make 201 appearances during one of the club's most exciting eras, scoring nine goals.  And such was his eternal popularity and standing, the great Nelson Mandela described Lucas as his hero.

### Lucas Radebe

**Clubs:**
Kaizer Chiefs (SA), Leeds Utd.
**South Africa Caps:** 70

# Shaun Goater

Shaun Goater was born in Bermuda where his mother Lynette was a former local football player. In 1989 during a break back at home from his football scholarship in America Goater was spotted playing football by a scout from Manchester United and offered a trial at Old Trafford.

Goater travelled to England and was offered professional terms but could not break into the first team at United and later that year he signed for Rotherham United. Over the course of seven seasons he scored 86 goals in 262 appearances and was a member of the Rotherham United team that won the Auto Windscreens Shield in 1993.

After seven seasons at Rotherham Goater spent two years at Bristol City before moving to Manchester City in 2003 for a fee of £400,000.

Goater managed 103 goals in 189 games as he helped drag Manchester City from a team in the depths of football's third tier to a team that racked up a record 99 points under Kevin Keegan to blast them back to the Premier League at the first time of asking.

During this memorable 2001/02 season Goater scored 32 goals making it his fourth straight year as their leading scorer and cementing his reputation as a genuine Manchester City legend.

'Feed the Goat' became a favourite terrace chant at Maine Road and it later became the title of Shaun Goater's autobiography.

## Shaun Goater

**Clubs:**
Rotherham Utd, Notts County, Bristol City, Man City, Reading, Coventry City, Southend Utd.

**Bermuda Caps:** 36

# Dwight Yorke

When Dwight Yorke joined Manchester United from Aston Villa for £12 million in August 1998, he became the world's twelfth costliest footballer and the second highest-priced player involved in a transfer between two British clubs. The very next month he equalled Chris Sutton's record by scoring what was then the fastest goal in the Premiership, after just 13 seconds for United against Coventry City in September 1998.

A lifetime buddy of the West Indian and Warwickshire cricketer Brian Lara and initially spotted by manager Graham Taylor, Yorke took time to establish himself at Villa Park. He made his League debut against Crystal Palace in March 1990 but had to wait until the 1991-92 season before gaining a regular place in the first XI when he made 39 appearances and scored 16 goals. Positive with neat skills and a penetrative approach, he was a natural athlete with great balance and a smart right foot!

A Trinidad and Tobago international with 72 caps and 26 goals to his credit, Yorke won the League Cup with Villa in 1996, three Premiership titles, the FA Cup, the Champions League and Inter-Continental Cup with Manchester United (being a key member of Sir Alex Ferguson's treble-winning team of 1999), Yorke also helped Sunderland win the League championship, Sydney lift the 'A' League title and his country to victory in the Caribbean Cup. He retired as a player in 2010, having netted 201 goals in 626 club games. His best years were spent with Villa - 98 goals in 287 outings - following up with 65 goals in 147 appearances for Manchester United.

Yorke - nicknamed the 'Smiling Assassin' - has a Level B coaching badge, and in April 2011 ran the London Marathon in three hours and 32 minutes. Four months later he signed a two-year deal to work for Sky Sport as a soccer pundit and soon afterwards agreed a deal with IMG-Reliance to take part in a proposed football League to be played in India in 2015.

DWIGHT YORKE

## Dwight Yorke

**Clubs:**
Aston Villa, Manchester Utd, Blackburn Rovers, Birmingham City, Sydney (AUS), Sunderland.

**Trinidad & Tobago Caps:** 74

# David James

Despite there being the fear that he was never more than a shot or cross away from dropping a clanger, David James' sheer presence between the posts added that little extra assurance to the defence of every team he played for.

He made his League debut for Watford against Millwall in August 1990 before moving to Liverpool for £1.25m in July 1992. His transfer fees in total eventually amounted to more than £9 million.

When he retired as a player in 2013, James had accumulated 944 club appearances. He had also gained five Youth, two B, ten U21 and 50 full caps for England, taking his overall tally to 1,011.

At one time he held the distinction of twice been the record holder for consecutive Premier League appearances, with 159 during his Liverpool days, 1994-98, and 166 while playing for Manchester City and Portsmouth, 2006-08. These streaks were eventually topped by Chelsea's Frank Lampard and Aston Villa's Brad Friedel respectively.

In February 2009, James set a new Premier League record of 535 appearances, eventually taking his tally to 572 - only Ryan Giggs and Frank Lampard have made more. Also the record holder for most clean-sheets in Premiership and Championship football (173), he won the League Cup with Liverpool in 1995 and the FA Cup with Portsmouth in 2008.

He was appointed a Member of the Order of the British Empire in the Queen's 2012 Birthday honours list for services to football and charity (he set up the David James Foundation in 2006).

James, who is an accomplished artist and is currently a regular pundit on BT Sport's football coverage as well as a columnist for The Observer, once pulled a muscle in his back when reaching for a television remote control and was forced out of matches. He also missed a match at Liverpool suffering from a RSI injury to his thumb which he blamed on his excessive computer-game habit.

## 'England's first black goalkeeper'

### David James

**Clubs:**
Watford, Liverpool, Aston Villa, West Ham Utd, Portsmouth, Bristol City, Bournemouth.
**England Caps:** 53

# Andy Cole

Andrew Alexander Cole was born on 15th October 1971 in Nottingham. He joined Arsenal's youth team at the age of 17 before signing professional papers a year later. He didn't get off to a great start at Arsenal, however, playing twice as a substitute in the 1990/91 season before being loaned out to Third Division Fulham.

Cole was soon sold on to Second Division Bristol City becoming their most expensive player at the time. During the 1992/93 season he became a regular goal scorer and was linked to a number of Premier League clubs. In 1993, he made a move to Newcastle United where he settled well and scored 12 goals in as many games helping to lift the Magpies into the Premier League. The goal rush continued with Cole scoring 34 times in 40 games and helping Newcastle to qualify for the UEFA Cup. Cole scored a total of 41 goals in all competitions in the 1993/94 season making him the highest goal scorer ever for the club.

Cole was unexpectedly sold to Manchester United in the middle of the 1994/95 season but despite the move, he still managed to score 12 goals in 18 appearances including scoring five goals in the 9-0 thrashing of Ipswich Town. Cole was the first player to ever score 5 goals in the Premier League. The 1995/96 season was more difficult as Cole struggled to fit into the team that saw Eric Cantona return. However, United still won the Premier League for the third time in four years.

Cole suffered with health problems in 1996/97 starting the season with pneumonia and then suffering two broken legs after a vicious tackle by Neil Ruddock in a reserve team match. He made a strong recovery next season and scored 25 times. His excellent work ethic and all-round skills helped Cole to be recognised as a strong all-rounder able to set up goals as well as score. In the 1999/00 season he passed the 100 goals mark for United but as the club acquired Ruud van Nistelrooy, Cole was no longer first choice striker and left for Blackburn Rovers in 2001; the first season saw him score 13 goals in 20 games for Rovers.

In his later career Cole enjoyed seasons at Fulham, Manchester City, Portsmouth, Birmingham City, Sunderland and Nottingham Forest.

Cole earned his first cap for England in 1995 and gained a further 14 international caps scoring one goal.

ANDY COLE

**Andy Cole**

**Clubs:**
Arsenal, Bristol City, Newcastle Utd, Manchester Utd, Blackburn Rovers, Fulham, Man City, Portsmouth, Birmingham City, Sunderland, Notts Forest.

**England Caps:** 14

# Darren Moore

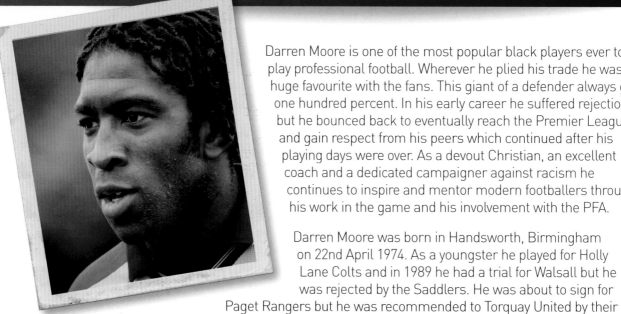

Darren Moore is one of the most popular black players ever to play professional football. Wherever he plied his trade he was a huge favourite with the fans. This giant of a defender always gave one hundred percent. In his early career he suffered rejection but he bounced back to eventually reach the Premier League and gain respect from his peers which continued after his playing days were over. As a devout Christian, an excellent coach and a dedicated campaigner against racism he continues to inspire and mentor modern footballers through his work in the game and his involvement with the PFA.

Darren Moore was born in Handsworth, Birmingham on 22nd April 1974. As a youngster he played for Holly Lane Colts and in 1989 he had a trial for Walsall but he was rejected by the Saddlers. He was about to sign for Paget Rangers but he was recommended to Torquay United by their Birmingham scout. He signed for them in June 1990 making his debut while still a trainee on 24th March 1992 in a 2-1 home defeat to Birmingham City. Darren turned pro in November 1992 and three years later he moved to Doncaster Rovers for £62,500 before going on to join Bradford City in June 1997. At 6' 3" he was ideally built for a centre back and he justified the fee of £310,000 by helping Bradford to promotion to the Premier League in 1999. He never played in the top flight for the Tykes because in November 1999 he was sold to Portsmouth for £500,000. He lasted just eighteen months at Pompey before joining West Bromwich Albion for £750,000 on 14th September 2001.

Moore proved to be a man mountain in the Throstle's defence as they gained promotion to the Premier League for the first time in 2002 and Moore was voted into the PFA Division One Team of the Year. Although relegated in 2003 Albion with Moore as their lucky charm returned to the top flight in 2004. In January 2006 'Big Dave', as he was known to the Albion fans (who had given him this name because of his likeness to a man in a TV ad for noodles), was sent off in Albion's 1-0 win at Wigan. It was his last match for the Baggies who subsequently transferred him to Derby County.

Ironically in May 2007 Big Dave was in the Derby side that beat the Albion 1-0 in the Championship Play Off Final. It was the fourth time Darren had been promoted to the Premier League and once again he was in the PFA Championship team of the season. Derby went down in 2008 and Darren was released, signing for Barnsley. He was there two seasons joining Burton Albion as a player coach in May 2010 serving alongside manager Paul Peschisolido. In February 2012 he left the Brewers and returned briefly to West Brom as a youth team coach. He eventually ended up as assistant manager to Michael Appleton in a brief but controversial sojourn at Blackburn Rovers which ended in 2013.

Since then Darren has pursued a career with the PFA and he has embarked on a number of Charity causes, including walking the Great Wall of China. He has received a number of awards for his charity work and contributions to football, particularly the Christian Charity, Faith in Football.

In 2014 Darren made a welcome return to The Hawthorns as a professional development phase coach.

## Darren Moore

**Clubs:**
Torquay Utd, Doncaster Rovers, Bradford City, Portsmouth, West Bromwich Albion, Derby County, Barnsley, Burton Albion.

**Jamaica Caps:** 3

# Sol Campbell

A central defender, strong, confident and durable, Campbell made a scoring Premiership debut at the age of 18 for Tottenham in a 2-1 defeat by Chelsea in December 1992. He spent nine years at White Hart Lane, captaining Spurs to victory in the 1999 League Cup final against Leicester City.

In 2001 he controversially joined Spurs' North London rivals Arsenal - the first high profile free transfer within the Premier League under the Bosman ruling.

In his five years at Highbury, he helped the Gunners win two Premier League titles and two FA Cup finals, encompassing the League and FA Cup double in 2002 as well as being part of the team that became known as The Invincibles for their undefeated season 2003/04 Premier League campaign. Campbell also played in the 2006 UEFA Champions League final defeat by Barcelona.

In August 2006, he joined Portsmouth and two years later skippered them to victory in the FA Cup final against Cardiff City.

Campbell who had a second spell with Arsenal in 2009-10, went on to appear in 644 games at club level (29 goals scored). He also won 73 full, 11 U21 and two B caps for England, and in May 1998, at the age of 23 years and 248 days, became what was then England's second-youngest captain, after Bobby Moore.

Campbell's only senior international goal came in the 2002 World Cup in the opening group game against Sweden. And in 2006, he became the only player to have represented England in six consecutive major tournaments, playing in the 1996, 2000 and 2004 European Championships, and the 1998, 2002 and 2006 World Cups.

Campbell's other honours in the game include being in the PFA Team of the Year three times, in 1999, 2003 and 2004.

## Sol Campbell

**Clubs:**
Tottenham Hotspur, Arsenal, Portsmouth, Notts County, Newcastle Utd.

**England Caps:** 73

Thierry Henry was born in Les Ulis, Essonne (a suburb of Paris) on 17th August 1977, where he played for an array of local sides as a youngster and showed great promise as a goal-scorer. He was spotted by AS Monaco in 1990 and signed instantly at the age of 13, making his professional debut in 1994. Good form led to an international call-up in 1998, after which he signed for the Serie A defending champions Juventus. He had a disappointing season playing on the wing, before joining Arsenal for around £11 million in 1999.

It was at Arsenal that Henry made his name as a world-class footballer. Despite initially struggling in the Premier League, he emerged as Arsenal's top goal-scorer for almost every season of his tenure there. Under long-time mentor and coach Arséne Wenger, Henry became a prolific striker and Arsenal's all-time leading scorer with 228 goals in all competitions. Henry first worked with Wenger at Monaco in 1994. The Frenchman won two league titles and three FA cups with the Gunners; he was nominated for the FIFA World player of the year twice, was named the player of the year twice, and the FWA Footballer of the year three times. Henry spent his final two seasons with Arsenal as club captain, leading them to the 2006 Champions League Final.

In June 2007, after eight years with Arsenal, he transferred to Barcelona for a fee of £24 million. His first honour with the Spanish club came in 2009 when they won the La Liga, Copa del Rey and Champions League treble. He went on to achieve an unprecedented sextuple by also winning the Supercopa de España, the UEFA Super Cup and the FIFA Club World Cup. In total, Henry has been named in the UEFA team of the year five times. In 2010, he joined the New York Red Bulls of the Major League Soccer series and won the Eastern Conference title with them in 2010. He returned to Arsenal on loan for two months in 2012.

Henry enjoyed similar success with the French national team, having won the 1998 FIFA World cup, UEFA Euro 2000 and 2003 FIFA Confederation cup. In October 2007, he surpassed Michel Platini's record to become France's top goal-scorer of all time. Henry retired from international football after the 2010 FIFA World cup.

Having been subjected to racism in the past, Henry is an active spokesperson against racism in football. The most prominent incident of racism against Henry was during a training session with the Spanish national team in 2004, when a Spanish TV crew caught coach Luis Aragonés referring to Henry as "black shit" to José Antonio Reyes, Henry's team mate at Arsenal. The incident caused uproar in the British media, and there were calls for Aragonés to be sacked. Henry and Nike started the Stand Up Speak Up campaign against racism in football as a result of the incident. Subsequently, in 2007, Time featured him as one of the 'Heroes & Pioneers' on "The Time 100" list.

Henry is the only player ever to have won the FWA Footballer of the Year three times (2003, 2004, 2006), and the French Player of the Year on a record four occasions.

## Thierry Henry

**Clubs:**
AS Monaco, Juventus, Arsenal, Barcelona, New York Red Bulls.

**France Caps:** 123

# Patrick Vieira

Arséne Wenger has brought many young players to Arsenal and turned them into superstars, arguably Thierry Henry is the finest example of that policy. Another great French player to blossom under Wenger's tutelage was a man who he did not actually sign but he was the reason why this brilliant footballer joined the Arséne Wenger French revolution at Highbury.

Patrick Vieira was born in Dakar, Senegal on 23rd June 1976. His family moved to France when he was eight. Patrick's grandfather served in the French Army which meant that Vieira was eligible for French citizenship from birth.

He played for Cannes as a 17-year-old, captaining them at 19. In 1995 he signed for Italian giants Milan but he was sold a year later. On the 13th August 1996 he moved to Arsenal for £3.5 million. Vieira joined the Gunners because he knew that Arséne Wenger was to become manager at Highbury.

Patrick made his League debut for Arsenal as a substitute in a 4-1 win against Sheffield Wednesday at Highbury on 16th August 1996. At 6' 4" he had a long stride and was a commanding figure in midfield. The press dubbed him "The thinking man's Carlton Palmer".

In 1997 the Gunners finished third in the league and Patrick won the first of 107 caps for France, against the Netherlands. The following season Arsenal won the Cup and League double, beating Newcastle in the FA Cup Final. In the summer of 1998 Vieira played for France who beat Brazil 3-0 in the final of the World Cup.

In 1998-99 Patrick was in the PFA team of the year as Arsenal were league runners up. They lost the UEFA Cup Final on penalties in 1999-2000 but by way of consolation Patrick was in the French side that beat Italy 1-0 to win the European Championships.

Arsenal won the double again in 2001-2002 after which Vieira was made club captain, succeeding Tony Adams who had retired. In 2003-2004 Patrick was captain as Arsenal regained the Premier League title, remaining unbeaten all season, a remarkable feat for Vieira and Arsenal.

His swansong at Arsenal came in 2005 when he scored the winning spot kick as Arsenal beat Manchester United on penalties after a 0-0 draw in the FA Cup final. It was his last goal for the Gunners.

Vieira left Arsenal for Juventus in a £20 million deal but quickly moved on to Internazionale where he won three league titles on the trot in, 2007, 2008 and 2009, as well as the Italian Super Cup. In January 2010 Manchester City took him to the Etihad Stadium and in 2011 he played the last game of his career as a substitute in City's 1-0 FA Cup final victory over Stoke. Patrick retired in July 2011. He now has a coaching role with the Blues youth team.

## Patrick Vieira

**Clubs:**
Cannes (FRA), AC Milan (ITA), Arsenal, Juventus (ITA), Inter Milan (ITA), Man City.

**France Caps:** 107

# Emile Heskey

Emile William Ivanhoe Heskey was born on 11th January 1978 in Leicester. He was a keen player from an early age and joined local youth team Ratby & Groby Juniors. He joined Leicester City's football academy at the age of nine and signed as a professional at 17, making his first team debut in 1995. He played 154 league matches, scoring 40 times for Leicester City.

Heskey signed for Liverpool on 10th March 2000 for £11 million for whom he played 150 times, scoring 39 goals. He also won the FA Cup in 2001. In 2002 Heskey was part of a consortium led by Gary Lineker to save Leicester City who were experiencing financial difficulties. Heskey personally donated a six figure sum to help the bid to buy the club.

Heskey moved to Birmingham City in 2004 where he was named Player's Player of the season as well as Fan's player of the season. In 2006 Blues were relegated from the Premier League and Heskey signed for Wigan Athletic for a club record £5.5 million. In 2009 he signed for Aston Villa eventually being released in 2012 and joining Australian A-League side Newcastle Jets.

Heskey began his international career playing for England at Under 16, Under 18 and Under 21 levels. He won 16 caps playing for the Under 21's and scored six goals. He also scored in his only game for the England B Team in 1998.

Heskey was called up to the England team in 1998, but did not play in the first game against the Czech Republic. His first game was against Hungary in 1999, followed by his first start for England at Wembley in 2000. Heskey continued to be part of the England squad even after the emergence of Wayne Rooney as a regular forward. He took over the captaincy from Michael Owen against Serbia & Montenegro in 2003 and it was their international partnership that led to Emile being capped further in 2004, 2005 and 2007. In UEFA Euro 2008, Heskey became the first player ever to be capped for England whilst playing for Wigan.

Heskey continues to play professional football for Newcastle Jets and remains a great inspiration for young black players.

EMILE
HESKEY

## Emile Heskey

**Clubs:**
Leicester City, Liverpool, Birmingham City, Wigan Athletic, Aston Villa, Newcastle Utd.

**England Caps:** 62

# Rio Ferdinand

Rio Ferdinand was born in Peckham and joined West Ham United where he made his first team deubut in 1996 as an eighteen year old.

With strength and good pace, impressive height and sound positional sense, as well as exceptional composure when in possession of the ball, it would not take long for him to become an established regular, and fans' favourite, as a quality central defender.

That same year Rio represented England at Under-18 level and then the Under-21 side the following season. His professional progress with West Ham was impressively and deservedly swift and he made his debut for the full England side, against Cameroon, in 1997, setting a then record as the youngest defender to play for England.

His consistently high performances attracted interest from the ambitious Leeds United who seemed desperate to make an impact in the transfer market. West Ham were eventually persuaded to sell their prized defender for a record-breaking fee of £18 million. He spent two seasons at Leeds and became the team captain in 2001, before Manchester United offered around £30 million for his services, making it two record-breaking transfer fees.

At Old Trafford he went on to win numerous club honours, including a championship medal in his first season as the club won the Premier League. Rio is still playing at the top level of English football and, in addition to his impressive collection of medals and silverware, and over 500 club appearances, he has represented his country 81 times.

Ferdinand is a vocal campaigner against racism in football, frequently making outspoken remarks about tackling racist and homophobic taunts from the terraces.

### Rio Ferdinand

**Clubs:**
West Ham Utd, Bournemouth, Leeds Utd, Manchester Utd, QPR.

**England Caps:** 81

# Clarke Carlisle

Clarke Carlisle was born in Preston on 14th October 1979, of Dominican descent, his father played semi pro football for Morecambe and Southport and from an early age it was clear that Clarke had his father's talent. He went on to be an accomplished player and also one of the most intelligent and articulate footballers ever to grace the game in this country.

Clarke gained ten A grade GCSE's and studied A-Level Maths and Politics at school but the lure of football took him to Blackpool in 1997 where he made his league debut as centre back for the Seasiders in Division Two in a 4-3 win at Wrexham on the 2nd of September 1997. After two years at Blackpool he moved to QPR in May 2000 for £250.000. He played three times for the England U21 side but his career at Loftus Road was marred by injury .

In 2002 Carlisle was voted Britain's Brainiest footballer after appearing on the quiz game "Countdown" On the field QPR lost the 2002 -03 Division Two Play Off Final to Cardiff City. The following season they gained automatic promotion. Clarke missed out on the glory, in September 2003 on the way to Colchester he was found to be under the influence of alcohol and was disciplined by Manager Ian Holloway. In June 2004 he joined Leeds. His stay there lasted twelve months.

Counselling and his Christian faith helped him to defeat his alcohol dependency and when he signed for Watford in the summer of 2005 his career was reignited. He helped Watford reach the Championship Play Off Final in 2006, a game which they won but he missed because of injury. Despite a loan to Luton he never regained his place in the Hornets side and on the 14th of August 2007 he signed for Burnley for £200.000.

Burnley had a fantastic season in 2008-09. Inspired by 6' 2" Clarke, the Clarets reached the League Cup Semi Finals and the Play Off Final defeating Sheffield United 1-0, Clarke was voted Man Of The Match.

On the 17th of November 2010 Clarke was elected Chairman of the PFA .His career however was winding down and after spells at Preston and Northampton on loan, Burnley released him in May 2012. Between 2012 and 2013 he turned out for York and Northampton before retiring on the 23rd of May 2013 having played his last game for Northampton in the Play Off Final defeat against Bradford on the 18th of May.

Clarke resigned as Chairman of the PFA on the 13th November 2013. Since 2009 he has enjoyed a career in the media. In 2012 he became the first footballer to appear on "Question Time" In the same year he presented a radio documentary dealing with racism in football and in July 2013 followed this with another programme on mental health in football. In June 2014 he joined the ITV team covering the World Cup in Brazil. He is still a regular church goer and he is an active member of the Kick It Out organisation.

## Clarke Carlisle

**Clubs:**
Blackpool, QPR, Leeds Utd, Watford,
Luton Town, Burnley,
Preston North End,
Northampton Town, York City.

# Ashley Cole

Hailed as one of the best defenders of his generation, Ashley Cole has played a prominent role in English football for the past two decades. In 1998 Cole signed his first professional contract with Arsenal.

On 30th November 1999 Cole made his professional debut in the League Cup. Although Arsenal lost 3-1 on penalties after a 2-2 draw at the end of extra time it was a significant step in Cole asserting his sporting prowess within the modern professional game.

As well as playing in the Premier League, Cole has also played for England both at youth and senior levels gaining a total of 114 international caps. After starting out in the Under 20s team, he moved up to the Under 21s and after just four games was into the senior team by the English manager - Sven-Göran Eriksson.

After his England debut on 28th March 2001 Cole became a regular fixture in the English side and is recognised as one of the top left backs in the world.

Cole moved to Italian club Roma in Serie A at the end of the 2013/14 season.

*'The first black player to achieve 100 caps for England'*

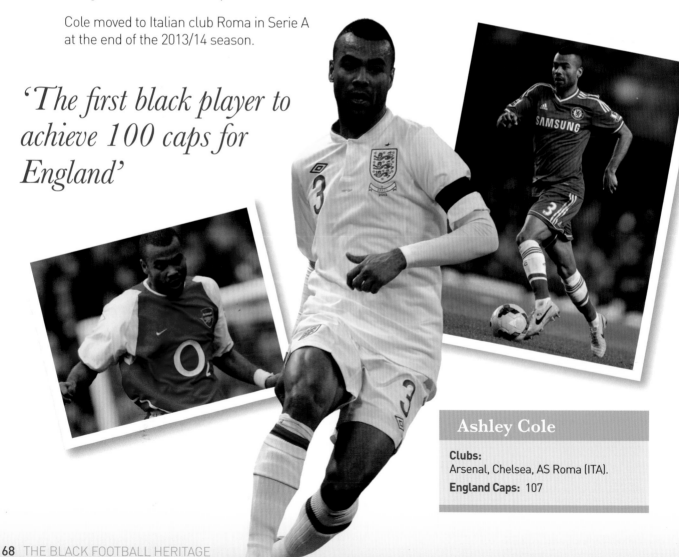

### Ashley Cole

**Clubs:**
Arsenal, Chelsea, AS Roma (ITA).
**England Caps:** 107

# Jason Roberts

When Jason Roberts was born in Park Royal, London on 25th January 1978, he had a famous uncle who was blazing a trail for black footballers in England. Cyrille Regis was playing and scoring goals for West Bromwich Albion in the First Division. Little did the Roberts family know but in time Jason would follow in his Uncle's footsteps and would enjoy a great career in football which would see him play for the Albion in the top flight. Like Cyrille he would receive recognition for his dedication to the game both on and off the field.

The young Roberts took up the game at the age of six and eventually played for the academy sides at Spurs, Watford, Chelsea and Wycombe but he failed to make an impression and he gave up the game for twelve months working as an export clerk. In 1995 his uncle Cyrille arranged a trial for him at Hayes, the club that had helped Cyrille on the path to stardom. Hayes signed Jason and in his first season they gained promotion to the Conference. In September 1997 he joined Wolves for £250,000 but never played a first team game for them and after loan spells at Torquay and Bristol City he moved to Bristol Rovers in August 1998 when Wolves recouped the fee that they had paid Hayes for him.

At Eastville he began to make a name for himself. The tall rangy striker was capped for Grenada and after two seasons in the West Country and 93 appearances, scoring 48 goals, West Bromwich Albion took him to The Hawthorns for a club record fee of £2 million in July 2000.

Roberts helped Albion into the Championship Play Off semi finals in 2000 and promotion to the Premier League the following season. Injuries and a stormy relationship with Gary Megson affected his game at the Hawthorns resulting in a loan period to Portsmouth in September 2003 and a transfer to Wigan Athletic in January 2004. At Wigan he formed a lethal strike partnership with Nathan Ellington which propelled them into the top flight in 2005. The Latics pair were chosen in the Championship team of the season.

Wigan consolidated their place in the Premier League and also reached their first ever major final, when with Roberts in the side they lost to Manchester United in the final of the League Cup in 2006. In July of that year Jason was on the move again signing a three year contract with Blackburn Rovers for £3million. During his time at Ewood Park in 2007 he started "The Jason Roberts Foundation" the purpose of which was to provide a range of sporting opportunities for children in the East End of London and Grenada. In January 2010 he received the MBE for services to sport in Grenada and London.

Jason Roberts made the last move of his career in June 2012 when after over 200 appearances for Blackburn he switched to Reading who were then in the Premier League. A hip injury caused his retirement from the game on 20th March 2014.

With footballing uncles such as Cyrille and Dave Regis, Otis Roberts and the Olympic athlete John Regis it was no surprise that Jason would be a successful sportsman. He continues to do good works and is a credit to his famous sporting family.

## Jason Roberts

**Clubs:**
Wolves, Torquay Utd, Bristol Rovers, Bristol City, WBA, Portsmouth, Wigan Athletic, Blackburn Rovers, Reading.

**Grenada Caps:** 16

# Fabrice Muamba

The story of Fabrice Muamba is one of triumph and near tragedy. In 1994 he fled war torn Zaire with his father to make a new life in England. As a football mad youngster he joined Arsenal embarking on a life in the game which he loved, little realising that his journey in the game would almost end in tragedy on a football field a million miles away from his homeland.

Fabrice Ndala Muamba was born in Kinshasa, Zaire (now the Democratic Republic of the Congo) on 6th April 1988. In 1994 his father left the country seeking political asylum, in 1999 he was granted indefinite leave to stay in the country. Fabrice was taken on as a first year scholar by Arsenal in 2002 graduating to their academy two years later.

He made his debut for the Gunners in a League Cup tie at Sunderland on 25th October 2005, Arsenal won and Fabrice played in the next round against Reading. In August 2006 Muamba joined Birmingham City on a season long loan. At 6'2" tall he had an all action style in midfield and people made comparisons with Patrick Vieira as Birmingham gained promotion to the Premier League and Fabrice was voted the Blues young player of the season. In 2006-07 Birmingham were relegated but not before Fabrice had made his debut as a substitute for the England U21 side against Romania at Ashton Gate in August 2007, the first of 33 caps at that level having turned down the chance to play for the DCR Congo in May 2007.

On the 16th June 2008 Fabrice signed a four-year contract for Bolton Wanderers who paid £5 million (plus an add-on of £750,000) for his signature. In his second season at the Reebok the Bolton News made him the Trotters player of the season.

Fate dealt Muamba a cruel blow when on 17th March 2012 he collapsed on the pitch at White Hart Lane in an FA Cup quarter final tie against Spurs. He had suffered a cardiac arrest. Fabrice stopped breathing for 78 minutes whilst he received treatment on the field, from, amongst others, a consultant cardiologist Spurs supporter who was in the crowd. Having had several defibrillator shocks on the field and in the ambulance he was taken to the London Chest Hospital where his life was saved. The game was abandoned and Bolton's next match at Villa was postponed.

Fabrice Muamba retired from football on 15th August 2012. In July 2012 he received an honourary Doctorate from the University of Bolton which he accepted on behalf of those staff who saved his life.

## Fabrice Muamba

**Clubs:**
Arsenal, Birmingham City, Bolton Wanderers.

# Daniel Sturridge

As a prolific striker for Liverpool and England Daniel Sturridge is one of the most exciting talents in the modern game. Born in Birmingham he first played for Aston Villa and Coventry before joining Manchester City in 2013.

He continued his development at City and played in two FA Youth Cup finals. He made his first team debut in the 2007–08 season, becoming the only player ever to score in the FA Youth Cup, FA Cup and Premier League in the same season. He left City in 2009 and signed for Chelsea, where he was loaned out to Bolton Wanderers for the second half of the 2010–11 season. After a successful spell at Bolton, scoring eight goals in 12 appearances, he returned to Chelsea for the 2011–12 season. He left Chelsea to join Liverpool in January 2013.

Sturridge has represented England at all levels. He made 15 appearances and scored four goals for the Under-21 team before making his full debut against Sweden on 15th November 2011.

Sturridge is actively involved in charity work, often helping young players get involved in football. In 2012, while playing for Chelsea, he presented a cheque for £50,000 to Street League, a charity dedicated to helping disadvantaged players across Europe get into football. In summer 2013, Sturridge opened his charity foundation in Portmore, Jamaica, with the aim of helping local youngsters get into sport.

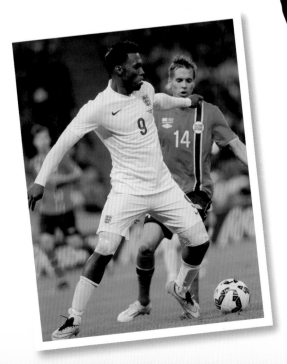

### Daniel Sturridge

**Clubs:**
Man City, Chelsea, Liverpool.
**England Caps:** 14

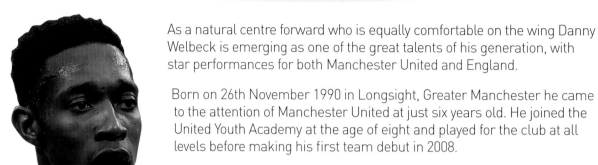

As a natural centre forward who is equally comfortable on the wing Danny Welbeck is emerging as one of the great talents of his generation, with star performances for both Manchester United and England.

Born on 26th November 1990 in Longsight, Greater Manchester he came to the attention of Manchester United at just six years old. He joined the United Youth Academy at the age of eight and played for the club at all levels before making his first team debut in 2008.

In 2010, he went out on loan to Preston North End scoring two goals in just eight appearances. He followed this with a further loan spell at Sunderland where he scored six goals in 26 appearances.

Since the 2011/12 season Welbeck has become a regular fixture in the Manchester United first team as well as for England. Ironically he made his full international debut in a draw against Ghana, the home country of both of his parents. His first international goal was the winner in a 1-0 victory over Belgium in 2012.

On September 1st 2014 (Summer transfer deadline day), Welbeck signed for Arsenal for £16 million.

**Danny Welbeck**

**Clubs:**
Manchester Utd, Arsenal.
**England Caps:** 26

# Raheem Sterling

Highly-rated by fellow professionals, managers and the media, Raheem Sterling had an excellent 2013-14 season in the Premier League helping Liverpool qualify for the Champions League with a second place finish. He was also called up for the full England team which resulted in a trip to the World Cup in Brazil.

Sterling was signed by Liverpool from the Queen's Park Rangers Academy in February 2010 by manager Rafael Benítez for an initial fee of £600,000, rising to £5 million depending on the number of first-team appearances.

In March 2012, he made his Premier League debut as a substitute against Wigan Athletic at the age of 17 years and 107 days, making him the second-youngest player ever to appear at senior level for the Anfield club.

In October 2012, Sterling netted his first competitive goal for Liverpool which was enough to beat Reading 1-0 and as a result he became the second-youngest footballer ever to score in a senior fixture for the Merseysiders - Michael Owen was the first.

Two months later, Sterling signed a contract extension, committing his future to Liverpool, and almost immediately he started to find the net in crucial games at crucial times while gradually drawing up an excellent liaison with fellow forwards Daniel Sturridge and Luis Suarez.

In April 2014, after producing some excellent displays in the red of Liverpool, he was named as one of the six players on the shortlist for the PFA Young Player of the Year award. And soon afterwards he was selected in Roy Hodgson's squad for the World Cup in Brazil.

## Raheem Sterling

**Clubs:**
Liverpool
**England Caps:** 5

# Saido Berahino

Berahino arrived in England in 2003 as a refugee after his father was killed in the civil war in his home country. He was 10 years old.

This incredibly difficult start in life has not held Berahino back for long; he managed to sign for the West Bromwich Albion Centre of Excellence in 2004 at Under 12 level. Looking to be a promising new talent for British football, the striker has enjoyed success on several loan spells following his professional signing for West Bromwich Albion in the summer of 2011.

Berahino made his professional debut for Northampton Town in October 2011 and scored a total of six goals in 14 appearances for the club. He then moved on to League One side Brentford for a further loan spell where he appeared seven times and scored four goals. This was followed by another successful period on loan to Championship Club Peterborough United.

He made his first League Cup debut for West Bromwich Albion against Newport County on 27th August 2013 where he stole the show by scoring a hat-trick. He made his Premier League debut for West Bromwich Albion in September 2013 as a substitute against Swansea City and soon after enhanced his burgeoning reputation by scoring the winner in a 2-1 defeat of Manchester United. Berahino has now secured his future with the Baggies by extending his contract until June 2017.

Since 2009 Berahino has been working his way up through the England youth ranks and in September 2013 made his Under 21 debut against Moldova. He has made no secret of his wish to join the senior England squad which should be a very achievable goal for a player with such promise.

Berahino is testament to the changing attitudes towards young black players in English football. He has carved a great start to what will undoubtedly be a very strong career in top flight football standing on the shoulders of black footballing pioneers.

**Saidho Berahino**

**Clubs:**
West Bromwich Albion

# Didier Drogba

Didier Drogba was born on 11th March 1978 in the West African nation of Ivory Coast. Although he has played for a number of clubs including Le Mans, Guingamp, Marseille, Shanghai Shenhua and Galatasaray he is best known for his achievements with Chelsea and his national side.

He is a supremely athletic, pacy, hard-working powerhouse of a player. His 100 goals for Chelsea in 226 games makes him the club's highest ever scoring foreign player and their fourth highest goal scorer of all time.

Didier made his professional debut aged 18 for Ligue 2 club Le Mans in France and by the summer of 2004 had moved to Chelsea for a club record £24 million fee. He is the most expensive Ivorian player in football history.

In his debut season at Stamford Bridge he helped the club win their first league title in 50 years, and the feat was repeated the following season. During his hugely successful time at Chelsea, he won the Premier League Golden Boot, managing to score the winning goals in League Cup and FA Cup finals. In 2012 he scored his 100th Premier League goal, the first African player to reach the milestone, and went on to become the only player in history to score in four separate FA Cup finals, when he scored in Chelsea's win over Liverpool in 2012. His last appearance of first spell at Chelsea was in the 2012 UEFA Champions League Final, in which he scored an 88th-minute equaliser and then the winning penalty in the deciding shoot-out against Bayern Munich.

His overall club career stands at in excess of 400 games played and over 170 goals scored.

Drogba left Chelsea at the end of the 2011/12 season but returned as a player coach in July 2014.

## Didier Drogba

**Clubs:**
Le Mans (FRA), Guingamp (FRA), Marseille (FRA), Chelsea, Shanghai Shenhua, Galatasary (TUR),
**Ivory Coast Caps:** 104

# Pelé

Edson Arantes do Nascimento was born in Brazil on 21st October 1940. He eventually became known as Pelé and grew up to become the greatest footballer the world has ever seen. As a black boy growing up in Brazil he saw poverty and hardship but football gave him the chance to escape from a life of deprivation. And it was football that helped him conquer the world.

Pelé exploded onto the world stage in 1958 in the World Cup Finals held in Sweden. He scored the winning goal in Brazil's 1-0 victory against Wales in the quarter final, a hat-trick in their semi final win over France and in the final he scored twice against Sweden to help the Brazilians carry off the trophy. As a shy 17-year old he became the youngest player to appear and score in a World Cup Final. He was voted the second best player in the tournament behind his team mate Didi.

Pelé became known as the Black Pearl and his fame spread worldwide. Brazil retained the World Cup in 1962 but he missed the Final because of injury. In 1966 in England he was the victim of some brutal treatment from Bulgaria and Portugal as Brazil failed to pass the group stage.

The greatest World Cup ever has to be the 1970 tournament in Mexico. Pelé was at his peak and the Brazilians assembled arguably the greatest team that football has ever seen. In the group stages they defeated England 1-0 . Pelé's tussle with the great Bobby Moore contributed to a truly memorable match. In the Final itself he scored  as Italy were crushed 4-1.

Pelé is the finest footballer the game has ever produced. He has inspired thousands of black footballers. On the field he was a master of his trade and off it he remains humble, dignified and respectful, a true statesman. In 1999 he was included in Time magazine's list of the 100 most influential people in the 20th century. A fitting tribute to a great man.

## Pele

**Clubs:**
Santos, New York Cosmos (USA).
**Brazil Caps:** 92

# Ricky Heppolette

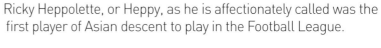

Ricky Heppolette, or Heppy, as he is affectionately called was the first player of Asian descent to play in the Football League.

Ricky was born in Bhusawal, a city north-east of Mumbai, India. He came to England with his parents as a three-year-old and settled in Bolton, Lancashire. Ricky, who just loved playing football as a child, was 15-years-old when he was spotted playing schoolboy football.

He was invited to Deepdale for a trial and soon signed up to be an apprentice for Preston North End in September 1964. Other clubs such as Southampton and Sheffield Wednesday had made offers to him but in his own words "he felt at home in Preston." He settled in well at Deepdale making firm friendships with John McMahon and George Ross, to mention just a couple. Ricky developed quickly, playing youth team and reserve team football. Eventually, on 20th April 1968, he made his Preston North End league debut against Middlesbrough, thus becoming the first Anglo-Indian to play league football. Heppy was super-fit, a real trier and the world just loves a trier. His love of the game shone through and he quickly became a firm favourite with the North End fans. Although the club was relegated from the Second Division in 1970, Heppy played a starring role in getting them promoted at the first attempt, as champions of the Third Division, under the management of Alan Ball Senior. Ricky continued to progress and won many admirers; if he lacked anything in natural skill, he more than made up for it in enthusiasm. After 175 appearances, in which he scored 13 goals, he was reluctantly sold to Orient for £45,000.

Over 40 years have passed since Ricky hung up his boots, but in spite of over 3 million Asians living in the UK, astonishingly there has only ever been three British players of Asian descent to have played Premier League football - former Fulham centre-back Zesh Rehman, Newcastle forward Michael Chopra and Swansea full-back Neil Taylor.

Other Asian players including Adil Nabi (West Bromwich Albion), Malvind Benning (Walsall), Danny Batth (Wolves) and Josh Sharma (Oxford Utd) are coming up through the ranks but how long will it be before they make an impact with clubs in the Football League or even the Premier League?

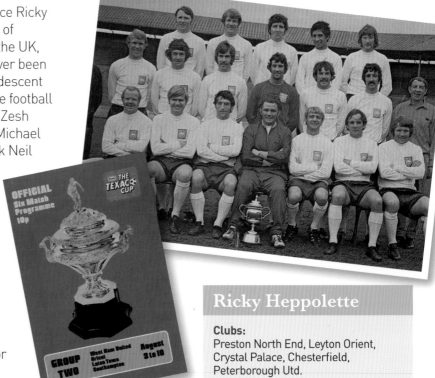

**Ricky Heppolette**

**Clubs:**
Preston North End, Leyton Orient, Crystal Palace, Chesterfield, Peterborough Utd.